KW-620-118

Authors in Their Age

MILTON

Esmor Jones

BLACKIE

BLACKIE & SON LTD
Bishopbriggs Glasgow G64 2NZ
450 Edgware Road London W2 1EG

© Esmor Jones 1977
First published 1977
Educational edition ISBN 0 216 90353 X
General edition ISBN 0 216 90370 X

W 4379 £1.95 1.78

All Rights Reserved
No part of this publication may be reproduced, stored in a retrieval system, or transmitted in any form or by any means, electronic, mechanical, photocopying, recording or otherwise, without the prior permission of Blackie & Son Ltd.

S. MARTIN'S COLLEGE OF EDUCATION
LANCASTER

Printed in Great Britain by
Robert Maclehose & Co. Ltd., Glasgow

4379
1.95
YGD
Milton

00022794

Authors in Their Age

MI

STACK

This book is to be returned on or before
the last date stamped below.

27. MAY 92

LIBREX –

B60672

Authors in Their Age

Authors in Their Age is a series of introductions to the work of major authors in English literature. Each book provides the background information that can help a reader see such an author in context, involved in and reacting to the society of which he was a part.

Some volumes are devoted to individual authors such as Chaucer and Wordsworth. Others look at a particular period in our literary history in which an author can be seen as representative of his time—for example, *The Age of Keats and Shelley* and *The Age of Lawrence*.

There is no attempt to impose a standard format on each of the books. However, all the books provide biographical material and deal with the important political, social and cultural movements of the time. Each book considers the author's readership, the problems of editing his or her work and the major influences on his or her writing. All are well illustrated with drawings, documents or photographs of the time.

There is also a guide to further reading and other source material which will enable the student to progress to a more detailed study of the writer's work and its treatment by literary critics.

Anthony Adams
Esmor Jones
General Editors

Contents

1	Towards a Biography	1
2	Milton's England	11
3	Milton and the English Revolution	24
4	Milton and Europe	37
5	The Milton Universe	43
6	Preparing for the Great Work	56
7	Paradise Lost and Regained	69
8	The Language of Miltonic Epic	84
9	Editing Milton	100
10	The Influence of Milton	106
Chronology		114
Bibliography		116
Index		119

I

Towards a Biography

At the time of the portrait by Faithorne, Milton was 62. The year was 1669—nine years after the Restoration of Charles II and two years after the publication of the first edition of *Paradise Lost*.

When we look carefully at this portrait we see that there is a solidity about it; in melancholy repose the face is clearly strong. The white collar, the dark clothes and the slight severity of expression suggest religion. It could be the portrait of a minister. It is certainly that of a Puritan. But the hair is long—Milton was no crop-eared Puritan—and the lips are full, almost sensual. The artist has given the eyes a kind of distant thoughtfulness, but this was a portrait the subject never saw, for at the time, John Milton had been blind for fifteen years.

1. Milton aged 62, by Faithorne (National Portrait Gallery, London)

Jonathan Richardson was a portrait painter who was only four years old when Milton was 61. But he spoke to men who knew him and reported what he learned:

> *I have heard many years since that he us'd to sit in a grey coarse cloth coat at the door of his house, near Bunhill Fields without Moorgate, in warm sunny weather to enjoy the fresh air, and so, as well as in his room, receiv'd the visits of people of distinguish'd parts, as well as quality. And very lately I had the good fortune to have another picture of him from an ancient clergyman in Dorsetshire, Dr Wright; he found him in a small house, he thinks but one room on a floor; in that, up one pair of stairs, which was hung with a rusty green, he found John Milton, sitting in an elbow chair, black clothes and neat enough, pale but not cadaverous, his hands and fingers gouty, and with chalk stones. Among other discourse he expressed himself to this purpose; that was he free from the pain this gave him, his blindness would be tolerable.*[1]

Here is another odd little portrait, this time from John Aubrey. They are just notes which Aubrey, a gossipy character writer of the time, never wrote up:

> *He was an early riser: at 4 o clock mane (in the morning). Yea, after he lost his sight: He had a man read to him: the first thing he read was the Hebrew bible and that was at 4½h+. Then he contemplated. At 7 his man came to him again & then read to him and wrote till dinner: the writing was as much as the reading. His daughter Deborah could read to him Latin, Italian, & French & Greek; married in Dublin to one Mr Clarke (sells silk etc) very like her father. The other sister is Mary more like her mother. After dinner he used to walk 3 or 4 hours at a time, he always had a garden where he lived: went to bed about 9. Temperate, rarely drank between meales. Extreme pleasant in his conversation & at dinner, supper etc: but satirical.*[2]

This is a glimpse, then, of the man John Milton at home in his declining years. He was still writing—*Paradise Regained* and *Samson Agonistes* were published in 1671—but he was living in a world he felt to be hostile, the world of the enemies of the Commonwealth. Richardson commented:

> *Besides what affliction he must have from his disappointment on the change of the times, and from his own private losses,*

> *and probably cares for subsistence, and for his family; he was in perpetual terror of being assassinated, though he had escaped the talons of the law, he knew he had made himself enemies in abundance. He was so dejected he would lie awake whole nights. He then kept himself as private as he could.*[1]

The second portrait was painted when Milton was 21. The year was 1629 and he had just graduated from Cambridge University. We can see the older man in the younger. The mouth is unmistakable and so is the long and rather elegant nose. The eyes are candid though the young man looks distinctly self-contained. A note from Aubrey reads:

> *He was of middle stature, he had light brown hair, his complexion exceeding fair. He was so fair that they called him the Lady of Christ's College. Oval face. His eye a dark grey . . . he was a spare man.*[2]

By this time, also, his poetic career was well started. In 1629, he wrote his 'Ode on the Morning of Christ's Nativity'.

We have two pictures then, at the beginning and towards the end of a dedicated, though turbulent, career. We know more about Milton's life than about earlier great writers. Whereas the biography of Shakespeare remains clouded in conjecture despite profound scholarship and the sharpest detective skills, there were biographies of Milton soon after he died. John Aubrey's notes were used by Anthony à Wood, who published in 1691, seventeen years after the

2. Milton aged 21, by an unknown artist (National Portrait Gallery, London)

death, when *Paradise Lost* had become accepted as a major work of genius. His nephew, Edward Phillips, published a life in 1694 while Jonathan Richardson's book rather later in 1734 included information he had garnered from men who had known Milton and from his descendants.

On top of that, there are quite extensive autobiographical comments in Milton's own prose writings. He was a political pamphleteer in tough political times and therefore concerned to establish his standing in the arguments. He talks most about himself, perhaps, in a Latin work *Defensio Secunda pro Populo Anglicano.* This second defence of the English people was published in 1654 and was part of a battle by pamphlet arising from the execution of Charles I. Milton strongly defended the killing of the King—hence his anxieties after the Restoration.

Milton's life falls into three parts. The first is his childhood, education and conscious preparation for his rôle as poet. The second covers the period of the English Revolution and his involvement with what seemed to him the epic happenings of his times. In the third part of his life, blind and mostly in the shadow of the Restoration, he wrote his three great poems.

John Milton was born in 1608, in Bread Street in London. His father had been something of a rebel. He had broken from the religion of his Catholic parents, been disinherited and forced to make his own way in the world. He became a scrivener—that is a professional writer of manuscripts, legal documents and so on—but retired as soon as he could. His chief interest was music and he was something of a composer: songs by Milton's father were still being sung well after his death.

It seems that John's father saw for his son what he had missed. Milton himself wrote:

> *I was born at London, of an honest family; my father was distinguished by the undeviating integrity of his life; my mother, by the esteem in which she was held, and the alms which she bestowed. My father destined me from a child to the pursuits of literature; and my appetite for knowledge was so voracious, that, from twelve years of age, I hardly ever left my studies, or went to bed before midnight. This primarily led to my loss of sight. My eyes were naturally weak and I was subject to frequent head-aches; which however could not chill the ardour of my curiosity or retard the progress of my improvement.*[3]

3. Christ's College, Cambridge. This is an engraving by David Loggan for his *Cantabria Illustrata 1688* and is a very accurate view of the college almost exactly as it would have been in Milton's time (The Mansell Collection)

EDUCATION

At the age of 12 he was sent to St Paul's School, though there was extra tuition at home. What he secured was a remarkable proficiency in languages—not only the classical tongues of Latin and Greek but also modern languages such as Italian and to a lesser degree French. To anyone interested in literature, Italian was more important. It was the language of the Renaissance.

Then, in 1625 when he was 16, he entered Christ's College at Cambridge. This seems to have been quite a disappointment to him. St Paul's, for its day, was a highly progressive school. To his headmaster, Alexander Gill, Latin and Greek were living tongues and poetry was the natural stuff of the classroom. Gill wrote a manual of English grammar (in Latin!) full of quotations from English poets—notably Spenser. At school Milton was made a member of an international culture, whereas at Cambridge he faced the antiquated and the parochial. He did not like it. The teaching system was medieval and based on a training in the logical and learned defence of a thesis. The trouble was the mustiness of the learning and the irrelevance of the topics. Milton was soon on the side of those who argued for radical reform:

> *Many a time, when the duty of tracing out these petty subtleties for a while has been laid upon me, when my mind has been dulled and my sight blurred by continual reading—many a time, I say, I have paused to take breath, and have sought some slight relief from my boredom in looking to see how much*

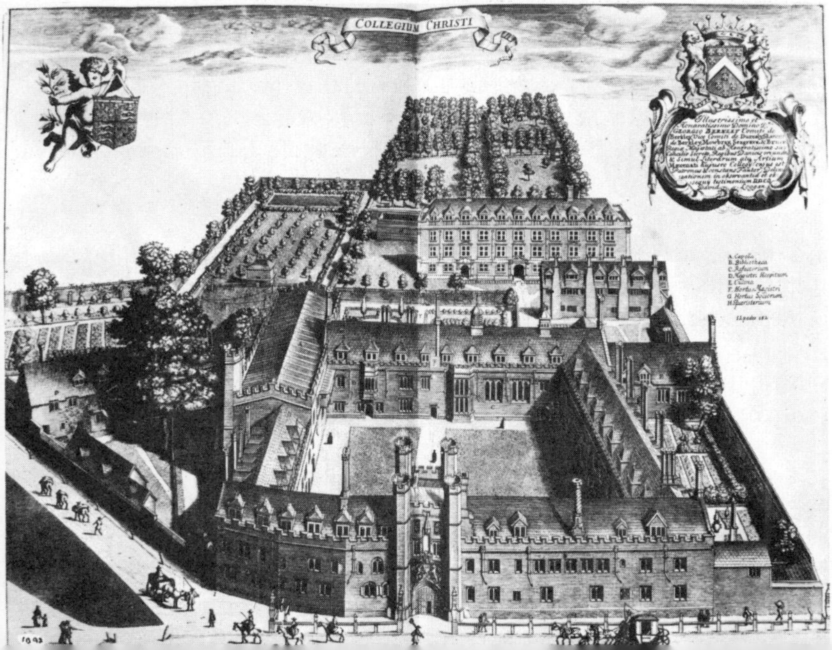

> *yet remained of my task. When, as always happened, I found that more remained to be done than I had as yet got through, how often have I wished that instead of having these fooleries forced upon me I had been set to clean out the stable of Augeas again, and I have envied Hercules his luck in having been spared such labours as these by a kindly Juno.*[3]

However, he did find time to write poetry, mostly in Latin, though there was a little in English.

A particularly interesting document of this time has the forbidding title of the *Third Prolusion.* It was, in fact, a public speech to his fellow students. He does not only attack the Cambridge system; he outlines what he feels would be an infinitely more vital education. He was, of course, fully conscious, at that time, of his destiny as a poet. *His* education must fit him for this task:

> *But how much better were it, gentlemen, and how much more consonant with your dignity, now to let your eyes wander as it were over all the lands depicted on the map, and to behold the places trodden by the heroes of old, to range over the regions made famous by wars, by triumphs, and even by the tales of poets of renown, now to traverse the stormy Adriatic, now to climb unharmed the slopes of fiery Etna, then to spy out the customs of mankind and those states which are well-ordered; next to seek out and explore the nature of all living creatures, and after that to turn your attention to the secret virtues of stones and herbs. And do not shrink from taking your flight into the skies and gazing upon the manifold shapes of the clouds, the mighty piles of snow, and the source of the dew of the morning; then inspect the coffers wherein the hail is stored and examine the arsenals of the thunderbolts. And do not let the intent of Jupiter or of Nature elude you, when a huge and fearful comet threatens to set the heavens aflame, nor let the smallest star escape you of all the myriads which are scattered and strewn between the poles.*[3]

This is a Renaissance enthusiasm—'integrated studies' in the humanities and sciences. The poet is a guide to knowledge, the inspirer of delight and curiosity.

Milton was not popular at Cambridge, neither with the dons nor his fellow students. The radicalism was too disturbing to the peace of the cloisters. Not surprisingly, he found few other young men who could share his intellectual concerns. He became a Bachelor of Arts in 1629 and then took his M.A. in 1632.

PREPARATION

After Cambridge began a long period of preparation. He went to live with his father in the small village of Horton in Buckinghamshire.

He had a plan of study at Horton, for it was certainly no gentle retreat from care and worry. He set himself to a comprehensive study of world history from the beginning, using all the authorities then known. One of the important consequences of this work was the settling of his political views and religious attitudes. There were breaks in study to write or to visit London.

During this period, he had one particular friend whom he had met at school, Charles Diodati, English but of Italian descent. Milton wrote to Charles in 1637:

> *Your method of study is, as I know, such as to allow of frequent breathing-spaces, visits to friends, a good deal of writing, and not infrequent journeys; while my disposition is such that no delay, no rest, no thought or care for anything else, can divert me from my purpose, until I reach my goal and complete some great cycle of my studies.*[3]

In a second letter, he shows something of why his studies had to be so strenuous:

> *What am I thinking about, you ask. So help me God, of immortality. What am I doing? Growing wings and learning to fly.*[3]

So now we have two of the major themes of Milton's life—the desire for immortality and the ceaseless struggle to achieve the goal. Milton's dedication and his constant effort of the will were quite extraordinary. Most of us experience a feeling of determination but only very spasmodically and perhaps over only a small part of our life and our concerns. What we have to imagine in thinking of Milton is of a man whose whole powers were directed day and night to the task of preparing for and writing *the* great work in the English language.

ITALY

After the long stint at Horton, he was able to make a trip to Italy. Italy was a great refreshment of Milton's spirit. The death of his mother gave him the freedom to travel. He left England in

April 1638 when he was 29, and was away for about fifteen months. First he spent a little time in Paris—largely so that he could meet Hugo Grotius, a lawyer and a pioneer in the development of international law. But he was not really interested in France; it was Italy he wanted to visit. He visited all the famous cities of the Renaissance, especially Florence and Rome. He spent some time in Naples. He came in contact with European artists and writers. He met Galileo. This visit made him a European figure as we shall see in greater detail in Chapter 4.

He returned to England in 1639, largely because he had heard of war between England and Scotland—the consequence of Charles I attempting to impose Anglican Bishops on largely Presbyterian Scotland. Milton wished to be nearer the action.

CIVIL WAR AND COMMONWEALTH

After his return from Italy, Milton took lodgings in London and began to teach a few children, starting with his two nephews. He wanted to be in London as it was there that Parliament met; there that Parliament had impeached Strafford and Archbishop Laud. It was in 1640 that he entered the war of the pamphleteers with a series of papers dealing with the Reformation and with aspects of church government. He was violently hostile to the bench of bishops and to the institution of episcopacy.

Then in 1643, at the age of 34, he married. It was a very odd affair. His wife, Mary Powell, came from Oxfordshire and was the young daughter of a distinctly pro-royalist family. But her father was in financial trouble and indeed had owed money to Milton's father at one time. Milton may well have met Mary during his period at Horton.

He was late in marrying. Earlier, his dedication to learning had kept thoughts of 'settling down' out of his mind. Indeed, he had toyed with notions of permanent chastity as more befitting a scholar and his destiny. But he felt strongly that marriage was a God-given institution and there can be little doubt of his strong feelings about women, and of his sensual nature, controlled as it was.

The marriage was a disaster. Mary went with him to London but returned home after a month on an excuse and, once there, refused to return to her husband.

Milton clearly had hoped for much from marriage and had been disappointed. It is difficult to comment further as we have little direct evidence of what went wrong. His nephew, Edward Phillips, who lived in the house as his pupil, says little in his *Life* save that the separation resulted in a series of pamphlets which Milton wrote arguing powerfully for divorce. This was not an orthodox viewpoint in the seventeenth century.

Milton's argument for divorce was not based, however, on self-pity but on an admission that he had made a mistake. This is what he had to say about his own feelings at this time:

> *And yet there follows upon this a worse temptation: for if he be such as hath spent his youth unblamably and laid up his chiefest earthly comforts in the enjoyments of a contented marriage, nor did neglect that furtherance which was to be obtained therein by constant prayers; when he shall find himself bound fast to an uncomplying discord of nature, or, as it oft happens, to an image of earth and phlegm, with whom he looked to be the copartner of a sweet and gladsome society, and sees withal that this bondage is now inevitable; though he be almost the strongest Christian, he will be ready to despair in virtue, and mutiny against Divine Providence.*[4]

What matters most from our point of view is the effect of this experience on his writings. Certainly, whenever John Milton contemplated matrimony or his own feelings about the other sex, there seemed to be unusual intensities and difficulties of control. His attitudes were ambivalent. There is at times a celebration of the delights of marriage, at times a celebration of the noble qualities of woman and also at times, an insistence that woman must be subordinate to man.

In 1644 he wrote further pamphlets—one on Education and the other the famous *Areopagitica*, a plea for the freedom of the press—at a time when he was feeling that Presbyterian intolerance was no substitute for Anglican (see Chapter 3).

Then in July 1645, in the middle of the Civil War, came a reconciliation with his wife Mary. At this time, Cromwell had just won the decisive Battle of Naseby. The Powell family were in deep trouble. Indeed, in 1646, Milton received the whole family in his London home as refugees. This says something about the kind of man he was; whatever the causes, Mary had made him suffer and the Powells were on the opposite side in the war.

There then began a particularly active period in his life. He wrote in 1649 *Tenure of Kings and Magistrates*, a strong defence of the execution of the King. This led to his acceptance of a government appointment in the Commonwealth régime as Secretary for Foreign

Tongues, and to further pamphlets in defence of the new order in Britain.

It was some time in 1651 that his sight finally went. A year later Mary died, leaving him with three daughters. By 1655, he was much less politically active—partly because of his sight and partly because he had completed his defence of the Commonwealth.

He married again in 1656. The evidence suggests this was a happy marriage but it was also a short one. Katherine Milton died in childbirth, as did the child, in 1658, the year in which Cromwell died.

THE LAST YEARS

Even at the last moment, Milton tried to prevent the inevitable Restoration with a pamphlet optimistically called: *A Ready and Easy Way to Establish a Free Commonwealth*.

He was briefly imprisoned in 1660; after all, as a defender of the 'regicides' he was a natural target for reaction. But he seems to have had friends (perhaps Andrew Marvell, M.P. for Hull and himself a poet of great distinction) and he was, by default, included in the royal pardon and left alone. In 1663 he was married for the third time to a woman called Elizabeth Minshull. She may have managed his domestic affairs efficiently enough but she cheated him financially. The menage of the blind poet had its oddities anyway. His daughters had little cause to love him. Without much of his ability, they were none the less obliged to serve his needs. He made them learn to read to him, as he wanted, in languages they did not understand.

This was the period of the major poems—*Paradise Lost* in 1667 and *Paradise Regained* and *Samson Agonistes* both in 1671. There was little immediate reward for them. *Paradise Lost*, it is true, sold over 1500 copies in his lifetime, for which he received £5. They were out of fashion with the age—an age of which Milton deeply disapproved. The fame came almost entirely after his death. He died in November 1674 and was buried in St Giles', Cripplegate.

[1] Jonathan Richardson *Early Lives* (1734) [2] John Aubrey (1681, Notes used by Anthony à Wood, 1691) [3] P. B. Tillyard *Milton, Private Correspondence and Academic Exercises* (C.U.P., 1932) [4] John Milton *The Doctrine and Discipline of Divorce* (1643)

2

Milton's England

John Milton was a Londoner. He was born in the City and spent most of his life there. Apart from his years in Cambridge, such time as he did spend in the country was within reach of metropolitan life. He had a cottage for a time in Chalfont St Giles in Buckinghamshire, and Horton was close to Oxford which, apart from being a university town, was virtually an alternative capital. The Government repaired to Oxford when there was the plague or the threat of it in London.

As you can see from the map (Fig. 4), seventeenth-century London was comparatively small and compact. Milton was born in Bread Street, a turning off Cheapside, close to St Paul's. He had several houses during his life—in Aldersgate, in the Barbican, in Holborn and finally at Bunhill Fields. They were all within half a mile of St. Paul's.

What London gave was bustle without and peace within a house. Here is a brief selection of contemporary impressions:

> *In every street, cars and coaches make a thundering as if the world ran upon wheels: at every corner, men, women and children meet in such shoals, that posts are set up of purpose to strengthen the houses, lest with jostling one another they should shoulder them down.*[1]

> *Now at London the houses of the citizens (especially in the chief streets) are very narrow in the front towards the street, but are built five or six roofs high, commonly of timber and clay with plaster and are very neat and commodious within. . . . The aldermen's and chief citizens' houses, howsoever they are stately for building, yet being built all inward, that the whole room towards the streets may be reserved for shops of tradesmen . . .*[2]

> *Paul's Walk is the land's epitome, or you may call it the lesser isle of Great Britain. It is more than this the whole world's map, which you may here discern in its perfectest*

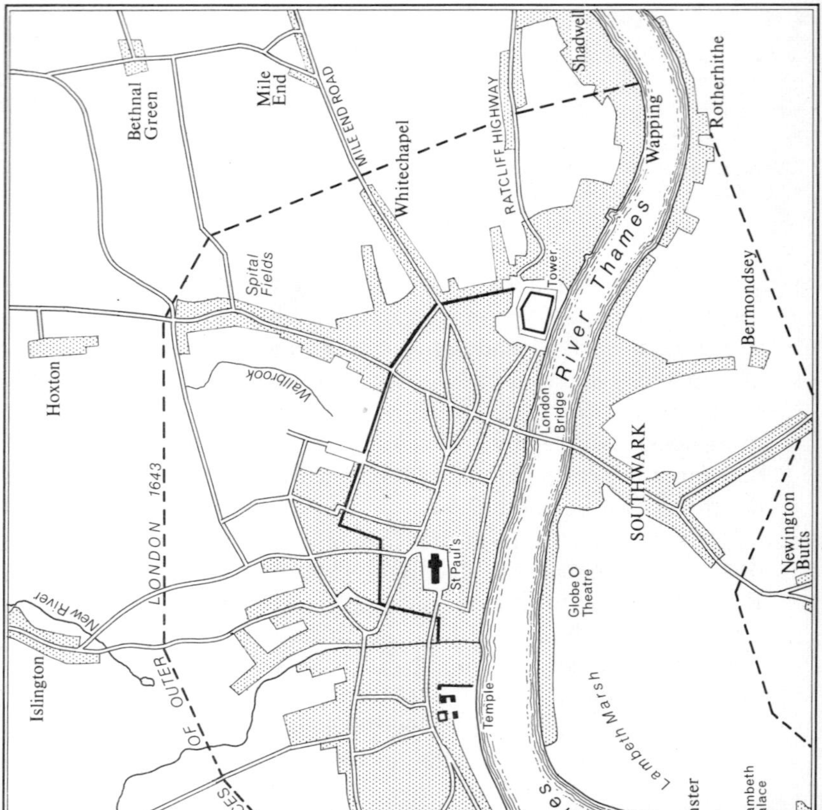

4. London in the mid 17th century (after Trevelyan)

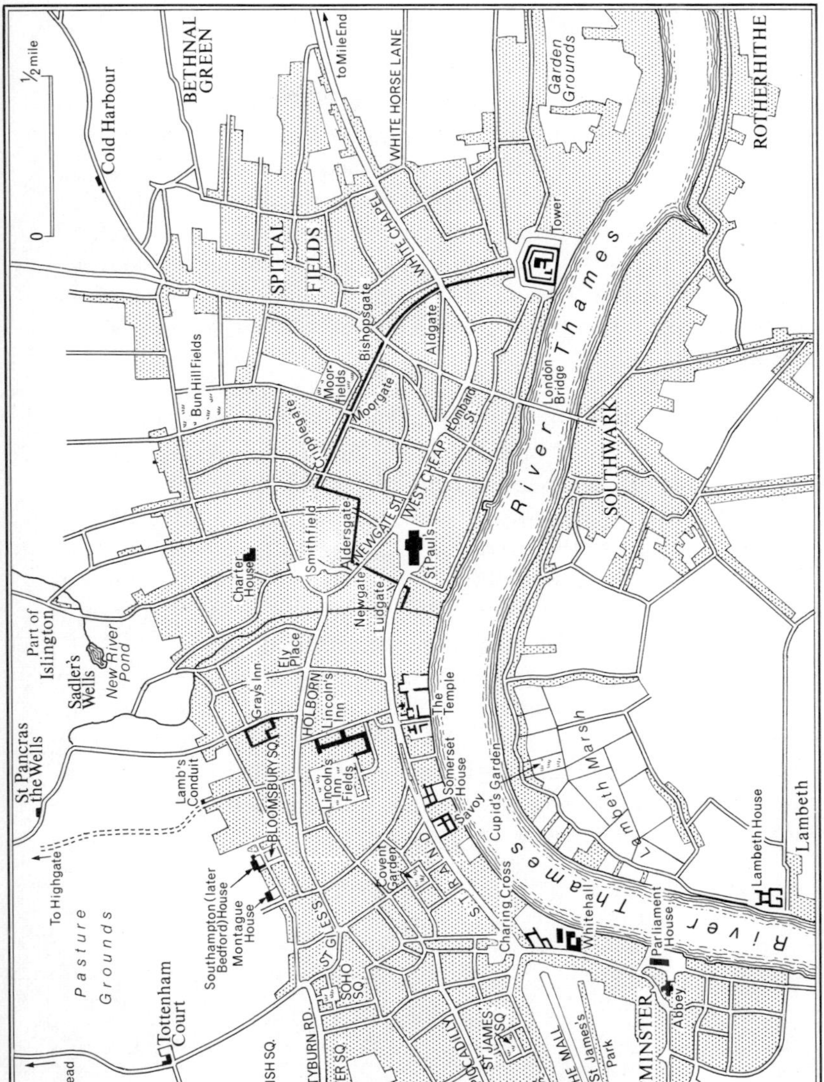

5. London in the early 18th century (after Trevelyan)

motion, jostling and turning. It is a heap of stones and men, with a vast confusion of languages, and were the steeple not sanctified, nothing liker Babel.[3]

It was a period of great growth as well. At the beginning of the century, London (including Westminster and the suburbs) had a population of 200,000 and was even then very much the largest city in the land. By the end of the century the population had doubled.

We talk today about the attraction of the south-east of England. It was true then too. The population of England and Wales was around 4 million in 1600. It had risen to $5\frac{1}{4}$ million by 1700 and out of these, one million lived in the Thames valley. This was Milton country.

As our population is now more than ten times as large, it takes some imagination to appreciate what it must have been like living in a country so thinly populated. If you have visited the ancient centre of one of our present towns where the old streets have not been pulled down for office blocks, you will also appreciate how closely huddled together were the houses and the people.

But the south-east was comparatively rich. More of the land was enclosed and farmed; there was less of the wild, a wild that people of the time found frightening rather than beautiful.

It was a country in a period of marked social change. The very growth in population suggests that. We may briefly note three particular forms of change here. There was a great shift from wood to coal, for timber was becoming scarce. Coal output increased fourteen-fold in the century, and this was not only for domestic use. Iron output grew as well. Secondly, a great deal of new land was brought

6. The City of London as depicted by C. J. Visscher in 1616 (The Mansell Collection)

under cultivation and the medieval strip farming diminished as landlords enclosed. It was in the seventeenth century that the Fens were drained and brought under the plough. Thirdly, as the growth in London suggests, there was a marked expansion in trade. There were increasing numbers of successful merchants. More and more young men found careers in government or in the law. As the middle class expanded in numbers, wealth and influence in the towns, so they bought land in the country. This resulted in a great broadening of the squirearchy.

Yet, in other respects, life was little changed from the days of Chaucer. How could it be with so few people? Christopher Hill puts it this way:

> *We should never forget how insecure life still was. Overseas trade faced the perils of piracy, shipwreck, the hostility of distant powers, scurvy etc. But life at home also was affected by natural catastrophes, the fires to which wooden buildings were so liable, unstable prices, arbitrary taxation, famine, pestilence, sudden and early deaths.*[4]

Milton knew many of these hardships from personal experience. He was in Chalfont St Giles in 1665 because of the Plague but back in London the following year—that of the Great Fire. His second wife died in childbirth. He suffered from price fluctuations and, as we shall note, taxation was one of the causes of the Revolution.

Christopher Hill continues:

> *The margin between success and failure was very narrow; a man might obtain a windfall by, for example, a prudent*

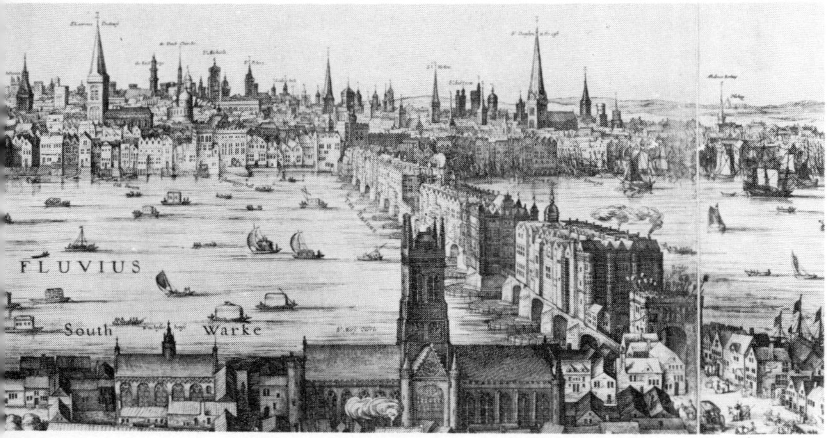

7. Milton's Cottage at Chalfont St Giles (British Tourist Authority)

> *marriage; but he could be ruined by factors quite outside his control.*[4]

This could be the story of the Powells. Certainly one reason that the Royalist squire married his daughter to the Puritan Milton was that he was in debt to Milton's father. The Powell estate was on the edge of bankruptcy, an edge over which it was pushed by the Civil War. It was not only as refugees but as bankrupts that Milton received the Powells in Aldersgate in 1646.

> *It is difficult for us, living in a world where everything is insured, where prices are uniform and not liable to violent fluctuations, where the weather is not a matter of life and death, where we can telephone for fire engines or the doctor and where expectation of life is more than twice that of the sixteenth century, to recapture the profound emotional instability of our forefathers. Naturally, they believed in theories of predestination (man's fate is in God's hands, not his own; success justifies). Naturally they wanted to propitiate this very relevant God—whether by ceremonies or by virtuous conduct. We should always take seriously the religious professions of sixteenth century men and women for many of whom eternity might seem much more real than this brief and uncertain life on earth.*[4]

What Christopher Hill says of the sixteenth century remained true in the lifetime of Milton with the added uncertainties of social unrest. Robert Burton wrote, with some degree of optimism:

> *We have besides many particular blessings, which our neighbours want, the gospel truly preached, church discipline established, long peace and quietness, free from exactions, foreign fears, invasions, domestical seditions, well manured, fortified by art and nature and now most happy in that fortunate union of England and Scotland which our forefathers have laboured to effect and desired to see.... Yet amongst many roses some thistles grow, some bad weeds and enormities ....*[5]

What were the weeds and thistles? There were three major sources of tension in early seventeenth-century England.

1 ECONOMIC

The following list of events suggests the increasing dependence of Britain on trade for prosperity:

i The expropriation of the monasteries and friaries by Henry VIII transformed ownership patterns and released capital.

ii For a number of reasons, trade moved north in the sixteenth century. The great new trading cities looked to the North Sea; they were no longer on the Mediterranean.

iii There was accompanying technical change which benefited Britain. As Carlo Cipolla notes in his classic study (*European Culture and Overseas Expansion*—Pelican, 1970) it was in Europe that men developed sailing ships that could tack and guns that could destroy. Rowing galleys could cope with Mediterranean coastal conditions. It needed the great ship with sails, gun deck and roomy holds to open up the trade of the rest of Europe.

iv The sixteenth century was the age of exploration. European ships reached the Americas. More profitably they explored the coasts of Africa, started the slave trade and reached India. By the beginning of the seventeenth century British merchants and British seamen were beginning to take full advantage of the new opportunities. We notice later the accompanying changes in the way people thought and felt about the world.

v There was more money available for new ventures. It was becoming a good period for private enterprise, for taking commercial risks.

vi Economic organization began to catch up with new needs. Characteristically, overseas trade was financed by groups of men in a company, each contributing share capital.

The economic opportunities beckoned on the growing middle class but the political system seemed to them a brake.

2 POLITICAL

What appears to happen is this. Gradually, for a variety of reasons, the ways in which people live and make their living change. However, the system of government usually does not change so fast. It is not very easy to change the institutions that we set up. You can see this quite easily in schools. For example, it can be very difficult fitting in a new subject in an old timetable. In the first half of the seventeenth century, it was becoming clear, to some people at least, that the form of government was no longer meeting their needs.

When James I came to the throne of England in 1603 and united personally the two kingdoms of Scotland and England, he inherited an only partly modernized system of government. He was an absolute monarch—yet there was Parliament. Elizabeth had had very little trouble with her Parliaments. Dutifully, they voted her the money she demanded; they endured her scolding when they showed any sign of independence.

The House of Commons that James summoned reflected the social changes. It was full of vigorous country gentlemen who were not afraid to speak their minds and who, increasingly, sought the power to control the affairs of state. There were a number of things which seemed to them wrong with Stuart government.

i It was arbitrary and thus unpredictable. James himself worked too much through favourites such as the greedy and incompetent Duke of Buckingham.

ii It was protectionist. Governments have often been like this, seeking to regulate trade, seeking to govern in detail how trade and industry was to be carried on. James raised money, for example, by selling monopoly rights and this was highly unpopular with the merchant class.

iii After the glories of Elizabeth, foreign policy was confused and disastrous. Attempts were made to find a Spanish bride for Charles. They proved highly unpopular. Negotiations failed and the country drifted into war first with Spain and then with France, ostensibly on behalf of European protestants. The wars were expensive and totally unsuccessful.

Much of this unrest came to a head in 1628. Parliament was summoned by the King to vote supplies for the war. They used the opportunity to voice their grievances first. They passed a *Petition of Right*. They complained about taxation without their prior approval, about the arrest and imprisonment of men without charge, trial or any proper legal process and about forced loans to the King and about the billeting of soldiers in large numbers on the citizenry.

> *They do therefore humbly pray your Most Excellent Majesty, that no man hereafter be compelled to make or yield any gift, loan, benevolence, tax or such like charge without common consent by Act of Parliament; and that none be called to make answer, or take such oath, or to give attendance, or be confined, or otherwise molested or disquieted concerning the same, or for refusal thereof; and that no freeman, in any such manner as is before-mentioned, be imprisoned or detained; and that your Majesty will be pleased to remove the said soldiers and mariners, and that your people may not be so burdened in time to come.*[6]

In effect, this was a drawing up of battle lines between Parliament and King. Charles dissolved Parliament and ruled for eleven years until financial necessity compelled him to turn to it again.

John Milton was only twenty at the time, in his final undergraduate year at Cambridge, where, in spite of the antiquity of the teaching, there was strong Puritan feeling.

3 RELIGIOUS

To many people, the central issue was not political but religious. The Reformation was far from complete. The Church of

8. The Kingdom of England (1627) by John Speed (British Library Board)

England compromise did not satisfy too many people. It certainly did not satisfy John Milton. Remember that his grandparents were Catholic, against whose religion his father had consciously rebelled.

The fortunes of the Anglican Church were closely associated with those of the monarchy. When James I was asked by Presbyterians to get rid of the bishops, he replied briefly and with a clear sense of the political reality: 'No bishops, no king'.

But what the Tudor period had taught many Englishmen was to fear Catholicism. In 1601, Thomas Wilson wrote, discussing the laws that compelled religious observance in the Established Church:

> *The main point is the weakening of the domestic enemies, for whereas the land is divided into 4 sorts of persons viz. (1) religious Protestants, (2) politic Protestants, (3) religious Papists, (4) politic Papists, the first whereof were only found to be sure to the state, the other 3 dangerous.*[7]

Charles I had a Catholic wife and, though he was always firmly an Anglican, the Stuarts were never free from the suspicion of being soft on the Papists. The Spaniards could return; the priests could come back and impose the terrors of the Inquisition and the stake.

The bishops were powerful men, closely involved, some of them, in the process of government. Church and state worked together to enforce the Act of Uniformity. While royal authority was strong, Archbishop Laud, for example, had the authority to compel the parish churches of England to follow his form of the Anglican religion, which seemed far too papist to the Puritans. At local level, in any case, the parish church too often served its people ill. Richard Baxter, a puritan writer, describes the village church of his Shropshire youth:

> *In the village where I was born there were four Readers successively in six years time, ignorant men and two of them immoral in their lives, who were all my schoolmasters. In the village where my father lived, there was a Reader of about eighty years of age that never preached and had two churches about twenty miles distant: his eyesight failing him, he said Common Prayer without book . . . After him another neighbour's son took Orders when he had been awhile an Attorney's clerk and a common drunkard and tippled himself into so great poverty that he had no other way to live.*[8]

Notice Baxter's reference to the old man with two livings; this was a constant source of complaint and not only about ignorant country clergy. People were often bitter about the habit of bishops retaining multiple livings to enhance their own income. But even more important to Baxter was the lack of preaching: '*The hungry sheep looked up and were not fed*'.

Here we begin to approach the strength of Puritan feeling. The movement stemmed from Calvin in sixteenth-century Geneva and was a root-and-branch rejection of Catholicism. At the heart of Calvinism was a belief in predestination. God had *chosen* before all time His Elect. Man is saved through Christ because God wills it so. Man is damned because God has foreknowledge of his sin and his non-election. In such a creed there can be *no* intermediary between a man and his God. The Elect know of their election through prayer, in the silence of the night. Even then, salvation and freedom from the consequences of sin do not come easily. Constant prayer, constant struggle are necessary. There must be unremitting attention to the Word of God, and that meant the Bible. To the Puritan, the Bible was a speaking book. By close study of its words, a man could hear the voice of God speaking to him.

It is difficult now to recapture the tough strength of Calvinist thinking, what it felt like to live thus in terror of the Wrath to come yet in hope of a personal salvation. It is perhaps most vividly and simply expressed in Bunyan's *Pilgrim's Progress.* Calvinism here has become absorbed into English rural culture. Christian is shown a picture of two children, one discontented and the other quiet:

> *Then said Christian to the Interpreter, Expound this matter more fully to me.*
>
> *So he said, These two lads are figures: Passion of the men of this world and Patience of the men of that which is to come; for, as here thou seest, Passion will have all now, this year, that is to say in this world; so are the men of this world: they must have all their good things now, they cannot stay till next year that is, until the next world, for their portion of good. That proverb, 'A bird in the hand is worth two in the bush' is of more authority with them than are all the divine testimonies of the good of the world to come. But, as thou sawest that he had quickly lavished all away, and had presently left him nothing but rags, so will it be with all such man at the end of this world.*
>
> *Then said Christian, Now I see that Patience has the best wisdom and that upon many accounts; because he stays for the best things: and also because he will have the glory of his, when the other has nothing but rags.*[9]

The imagery of *Pilgrim's Progress* is very old—life as a journey, a very temporary affair. But to the Puritan, the manner of the journey was everything. Bishops and, indeed, kings, beckoned off the straight and narrow path. The great historian R. H. Tawney comments:

> *Overwhelmed by a sense of his Ultimate End, the Puritan cannot rest, nevertheless, in reflection upon it. The contemplation of God . . . is a blessedness too great for sinners, who must not only contemplate God, but glorify him by their work in a world given over to the powers of darkness. 'The way to the Celestial City lies just through this town, where this lusty fair is kept, and he that will go to the City, and yet not go through this town, must needs go out of the world'. For that awful journey, girt with precipices and beset with fiends, he sheds every encumbrance and arms himself with every weapon. . . . He seeks from his ministers, not absolution, but instruction, exhortation and warning. . . . He disciplines, rationalizes, systematizes his life, 'method' was a Puritan catchword before the world had thought of Methodists. He makes his very business a travail of the spirit, for that too is the Lord's vineyard, in which he is called to labour.*
>
> *Feeling in him that which 'maketh him more fearful of displeasing God than all the world'* (Baxter) *he is a natural republican, for there is none on earth he can own as master. If powers and principalities will hear and obey, well; if not, they must be ground into dust, that on their ruins the elect may build the Kingdom of Christ.*[10]

As Tawney says, the essence of Puritanism is *will* and it is this, pre-eminently, that puts Milton among the Puritans. As we shall see, he was by no means the conventional Puritan of his time; he certainly did not share all of Calvinist doctrine. But he has the same sense of the world to come, the same indomitable will, the same independence of spirit, the same loneliness before God.

No such religion would make the headway that Calvinism did unless it met deep human needs at the time. We have already noted a relationship between insecurity and a sense of another world. As the old feudalism weakened and towns grew in importance so a religion which made sense of individual experience rather than stressed the social order seemed more satisfying. As Tawney says again:

> *To contemporaries the chosen seat of the Puritan spirit seemed to be those classes in society which combined economic inde-*

> *pendence, education, and a certain decent pride in their status, revealed at once in a determination to live their own lives, without truckling to earthly superiors, and in a somewhat arrogant contempt for those, who, either through weakness of character or through economic helplessness, were less resolute, less vigorous and masterful than themselves.*[10]

So Puritan objection to the Established Church reinforced the new feelings of the middle classes, the desire to be done with ancient restraints upon work and to secure a proper self-government. An insistence upon the right of a church to organize itself free from the interference of the State inevitably went hand in hand with an insistence on civil liberties.

Of his attackers, Milton wrote:

> *But since my enemies boast that this affliction (blindness) is only a retribution for the transgressions of my pen, I again invoke the Almighty to witness, that I never, at any time, wrote anything which I did not think agreeable to truth, justice and to piety. This was my persuasion then, and I feel the same persuasion now. Nor was I ever prompted to such exertions by the influence of ambition, by the lust of lucre or of praise; it was only by the conviction of duty and the feeling of patriotism, a disinterested passion for the extension of civil and religious liberty.*[11]

Elsewhere in a famous passage he wrote:

> *I cannot praise a fugitive and cloistered virtue, unexercised and unbreathed, that never sallies out and sees her adversary, but slinks out of the race, where that immortal garland is to be run for, not without dust and heat.*[12]

[1] Thomas Dekker *The Seven Deadly Sins of London* (1606) [2] Fynes Moryson *Itinerary* (1617) [3] John Earle *Microcosmographie* (1628) [4] Christopher Hill *Reformation to Industrial Revolution* (Penguin, 1969) [5] Robert Burton *Anatomy of Melancholy* (1621) [6] *Petition of Right* (1628) [7] Thomas Wilson *The State of England* (1601) [8] Richard Baxter *Reliquiae Baxterianae* (1696) [9] John Bunyan *The Pilgrim's Progress* (1678) [10] R. H. Tawney *Religion and the Rise of Capitalism* (Murray, 1926; also Penguin) [11] John Milton *Defensio Secunda pro Populo Anglicano* (1654) [12] Milton *Areopagitica* (1644)

3

Milton and the English Revolution

In 1639, Charles I found himself embroiled in war with Scotland. Foolishly, he and Archbishop Laud had attempted to impose on the largely Presbyterian Scots the Anglican system of Bishops and the Book of Common Prayer.

This was the year when John Milton was in Italy. When he heard the news, he knew that great events might be in the offing. He cut short his stay and hurried back to be closer to whatever was to happen. Events did move fast. The war was an expensive farce. Charles ran out of money and was compelled, after eleven years of managing without, to call a parliament.

When Parliament assembled, it was clearly in a dangerous mood. There was to be no money for a Bishops' War in Scotland without far-reaching reforms in the kingdom of England. Charles dismissed this troublesome Parliament after a fortnight. A further attempt to impose Anglicanism on Scotland by force was a further dismal failure. Charles was forced in November of 1640 to call another parliament. This was the Long Parliament, the Parliament of the Civil War.

From the first, Milton was deeply involved in these events. When the opportunity came, it was natural for him to use his talents actively for the cause in which he believed. In a sense, the Civil War and the Commonwealth were an interruption to his career as a poet. Certainly, the kind of great poem he wished to write changed as his hopes for England rose and fell. But it was also part of the period of preparation that would fit him for the great scheme of *Paradise Lost* and *Paradise Regained*. It was no cliché to Milton to feel that he lived in epic times.

FREEDOM

The seventeenth century was not a period in which freedom, as we think we know it, was felt to be the proper condition of life. The age-old analogy of the state as a body remained powerful in the minds of most men. If we were all members one of another, each

9. The three faces of Laud, Archbishop of Canterbury: the Bible, the Service Book, Superstition.

The least of these the greatest ought to be;
The other two, of Man and of the Devil,
Ought to be rooted out for e'er as evil.

(Radio Times Hulton Picture Library)

with his appointed rôle, then there had to be unity in all things and especially in religion. It was not only the Catholics of the time who felt that to cleave to a different religion, to be a heretic, was to threaten the health of state and people.

After all, the Church of England, though very much a compromise, had stood in its own way for England. England had survived attempted invasion from Catholic Spain. We should not be surprised at the strength of feeling against the Catholics and in favour of religious uniformity. There were a number of reasons for Charles having made the mistake of attacking Scotland in 1639 and again in 1640. Undoubtedly, though, the most powerful was this desire to see everyone united in the same faith.

Naturally, the various parties of the Puritans—Presbyterians and Independents—felt differently. They desired liberty for themselves to worship as they thought right. This liberty, however, could well be a liberty to impose a new uniformity. What distinguished Anglican from Presbyterian was theology and a different conception of church government. Both parties shared the view that all men should worship together in the same church. Later Milton was to comment acidly: '*New Presbyter is but old priest writ large*'.

In practice, the government of Cromwell allowed a considerable degree of religious toleration. It had to. There were too many sects among the Puritans and there was too strong a resistance to the attempt of the Presbyterians to impose their forms upon the new state. Here is the article from the 1653 *Instrument of Government* that deals with toleration. Notice the limits; the article was framed to exclude not only Catholics and Anglicans but also certain extreme Protestant sects (Ranters, Quakers, and such like).

> *That such as profess faith in God by Jesus Christ (though differing in judgement from the doctrine, worship or discipline publicly held forth) shall not be restrained from, but shall be protected in, the profession of the faith and exercise of their religion; so as they abuse not this liberty to the civil injury of others and to the actual disturbance of the public peace on their parts: provided this liberty be not extended to popery nor prelacy, nor to such as, under the profession of Christ, hold forth and practice licentiousness.*[1]

At first John Milton supported the Presbyterian point of view. He was certainly strongly hostile to bishops. He entered the pamphlet war, which was one of the most striking features of the period. Printing had become fairly cheap and paper was readily available. Hundreds of pamphlets were written from every conceivable point of view. A good and forceful controversialist was an asset to one's party. In 1641, Milton wrote two such pamphlets attacking the episcopacy. This was the year in which the House of Commons demanded an end to bishops and impeached Archbishop Laud.

Milton summarized his reasons for disliking bishops thus:

> *If the religion be pure, spiritual, simple and lowly, as the gospel most truly is, such must the face of the ministry be. And in like manner if the form of the ministry be grounded in the worldly degrees of authority, honour, temporal jurisdiction, we see it with our eyes it will turn the inward power and purity of the gospel into the outward carnality of the law; evaporating and exhaling the internal worship into empty conformities and gay shows.*[2]

Notice towards the end the key word 'internal'. We are at the heart of the Puritan position—grace operates in the hearts of man. All else is show. In *The Pilgrim's Progress* Mr Legality would have led Christian to damnation. Milton wrote:

> *Under the gospel we possess, as it were, a twofold scripture: one external, which is the written word; and the other*

> *internal, which is the Holy Spirit, written in the hearts of believers.*[3]

This is taken from *De Doctrina Christiana* (*Christian Doctrine*), a remarkable if somewhat unreadable work in which Milton endeavours to lay out in detail what he takes to be Christian doctrine as it can be teased out from deep study of the scriptures. The very business of wrestling with the word of God to seek out His way to salvation was characteristic of Puritanism. What distinguished Milton was an unusual learning and thoroughness.

By this time, Milton's own notion of freedom was beginning to differ from the norm. The bounded liberty of the 1653 *Instruments of Government* began in Milton's mind to become much less constrained, though he was never to admit toleration to papists:

> *Every believer has a right to interpret the scriptures for himself, inasmuch as he has the Spirit for his guide, and the mind of Christ is in him.*[3]

At such a time, such a view obviously has political implications. Opposing the bishops led to opposing the King—for rather similar reasons. There is much in the Bible about bad kings (glance through the Books of Kings and Chronicles). After all, as the 8th chapter of the 1st Book of Samuel makes clear, there was religious disapproval of the Israelites' desire for a king. In *Paradise Lost* Milton states the case like this:

> *Since thy original lapse, true Libertie*
> *Is lost, which alwayes with right Reason dwells*
> *Twinnd, and from her hath no dividual being:*
> *Reason in man obscur'd, or not obeyd,*
> *Immediatly inordinate desires*
> *And upstart Passions catch the Goverment*
> *From Reason, and to servitude reduce*
> *Man till then free. Therefore since hee permits*
> *Within himself unworthie Powers to reign*
> *Over free Reason, God, in Judgement just*
> *Subjects him from without to violent Lords;*
> *Who oft as undeservedly enthrall*
> *His outward freedom: Tyrannie must be,*
> *Though to the Tyrant thereby no excuse.*[4]

Charles was just such a 'violent Lord'; however inevitable in a fallen nation, notice the Tyrant is not excused.

John Milton's main defence of freedom is in a pamphlet called *Areopagitica*, which was published in November 1644. This was shortly after the first major Parliamentary victory of the Civil War at Marston Moor. The pamphlet was a powerful plea for freedom of the press. Right from the days of Elizabeth, printing had been controlled. A book had to have a royal licence to be published. The Company of Stationers, too, had a monopoly of printing. In 1641, when the Long Parliament abolished the royal court—the Star Chamber—which controlled licensing, they put nothing in its place. So for a time there was, accidentally, complete freedom to print and publish. A number of unofficial presses sprang up. The Company of Stationers, alarmed at the threat to their monopoly, petitioned for the return of licensing. So Parliament, horrified anyway at all the heretical and seditious material that was pouring out, duly obliged, though Milton got away quite easily with publishing unlicensed pamphlets. The ones on Divorce are an example. *Areopagitica* was written then to oppose any renewal of licensing (or censorship). It was also an attack on Presbyterian intolerance, and an assertion of a doctrine that ran counter to the Calvinist belief in predestination. Milton asserted what had come to be his own belief in free will. It is an argument that is at the heart of *Paradise Lost*.

Here, then, are some key passages from *Areopagitica*.

> *For books are not absolutely dead things, but do contain a potency of life in them to be as active as that soul was whose progeny they are; nay they do preserve as in a vial the purest efficacy and extraction of that living intellect that bred them. I know they are as lively, and as vigorously productive, as those fabulous Dragon's teeth; and being sown up and down, may chance to spring up armed men. And yet on the other hand unless wariness be used, as good almost kill a Man as kill a good book; who kills a Man kills a reasonable creature, God's image; but he who destroys a good Book, kills reason itself, kills the Image of God, as it were in the eye.*[5]

> *Good and evil we know in the field of this world grow up together almost inseperably; and the knowledge of good is so involved and interwoven with the knowledge of evil, and in so many cunning resemblances hardly to be discerned, that those confused seeds that were imposed on Psyche as an incessant labour to cull out, and sort asunder, were not more intermixed. It was from out the rind of one apple tasted, that the*

knowledge of good and evil, as two twins cleaving together, leaped forth into the world. And perhaps this is that doom which Adam fell into of knowing good and evil; that is to say, of knowing good by evil. As therefore the state of man now is; what wisdom can there be to choose, what continence to forbear, without the knowledge of evil?[5]

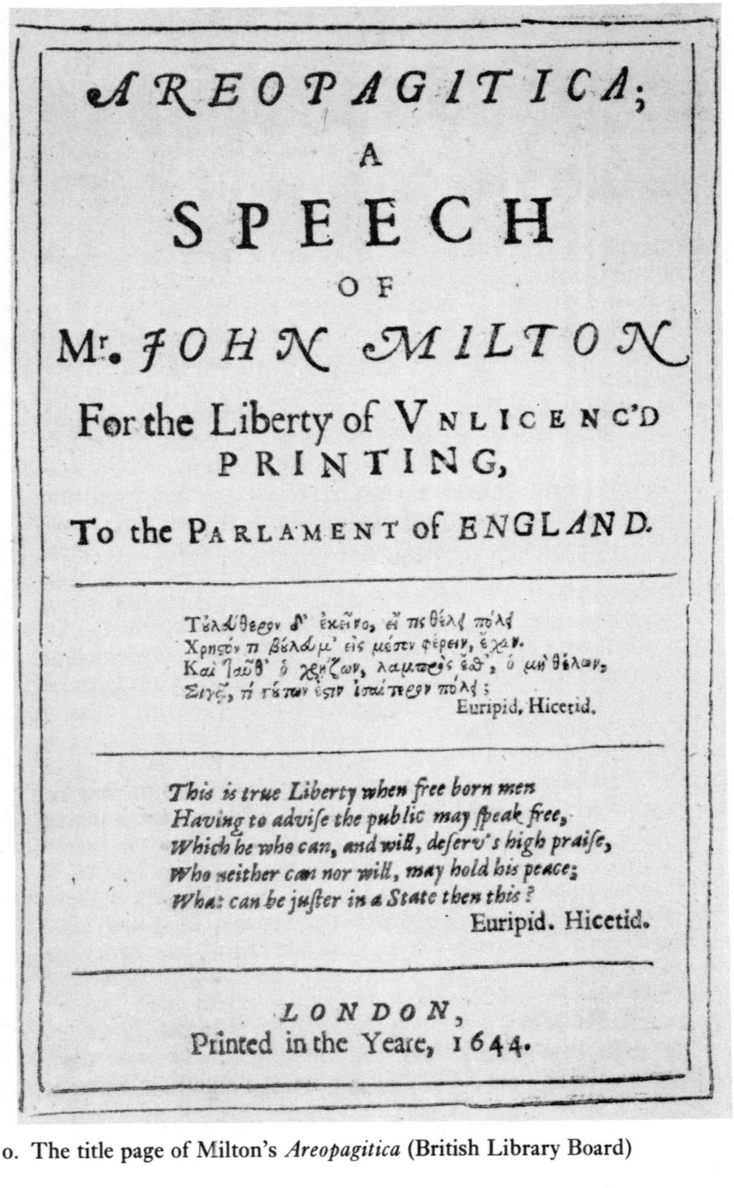

AREOPAGITICA;
A
SPEECH
OF
Mr. *JOHN MILTON*
For the Liberty of UNLICENC'D
PRINTING,
To the PARLAMENT of *ENGLAND.*

Τοὐλεύθερον δ' ἐκεῖνο, εἴ τις θέλει πόλει
Χρηστόν τι βούλευμ' εἰς μέσον φέρειν, ἔχων.
Καὶ ταῦθ' ὁ χρῄζων, λαμπρὸς ἔσθ', ὁ μὴ θέλων,
Σιγᾷ, τί τούτων ἔστιν ἰσαίτερον πόλει;
Euripid, Hicetid.

This is true Liberty when free born men
Having to advise the public may speak free,
Which he who can, and will, deserv's high praise,
Who neither can nor will, may hold his peace;
What can be juster in a State then this?
Euripid. Hicetid.

LONDON,
Printed in the Yeare, 1644.

10. The title page of Milton's *Areopagitica* (British Library Board)

> *Many there be that complain of divine Providence for suffering Adam to transgress, foolish tongues! when God gave him Reason, he gave him freedom to choose, for reason is but choosing.*[5]

> *Suppose we could expel sin by this means* (i.e. licensing of books)*; look how much we thus expel of sin, so much we expel of virtue: for the matter of them both is the same; remove that and ye remove them both alike. This justifies the high Providence of God, who though he commands us temperance, justice, continence, yet pours out before us even to a profuseness all desirable things, and gives us minds that can wander beyond all limit and satiety.*[5]

THE MILLENNIUM

From 1640 to 1660 Milton must have felt, at the time partly and in retrospect wholly, as if he were an actor living through a great and terrible drama. It was epic turned tragedy. As we shall see, *Paradise Lost* was conceived and largely planned during this period. But it was written *after* the Restoration. It was written after Milton had become blind, after he had, as he must have felt, given his eyesight to the cause. To understand the disappointment of hopes, we must appreciate the hopes themselves.

All religions thrive on promised hope. The hope or salvation may be in another world. But it can be in this. There are texts in the Bible (notably in the prophetic works and in such apocalyptic works as Daniel and Revelation) that suggest that in his own time the Lord will establish his reign upon the earth.

There was to be an Antichrist (readily identified as the Pope) who would rule the earth, but the time would come (marked by many marvels) when Christ himself would come again and establish His Kingdom on earth and reign with His Saints. Here is the beginning to chapter 20 of the Book of Revelation:

> *And I saw an angel come down from heaven, having the key of the bottomless pit and a great chain in his hand.*
>
> *And he laid hold on the dragon, that old serpent, which is the Devil, and Satan, and bound him a thousand years.*
>
> *And cast him into the bottomless pit, and shut him up and set a seal upon him that he should deceive the nations no more, till the thousand years should be fulfilled: and after that he must be loosed a little season.*

And I saw thrones and they sat upon them and judgement was given unto them: and I saw the souls of them that were beheaded for the witness of Jesus, and for the word of God, and which had not worshipped the beast, neither his image, neither had received his mark upon their foreheads, or in their hands; and they lived and reigned with Christ a thousand years.

But the rest of the dead lived not again until the thousand years were finished. This is the first resurrection.[6]

The scripture is not easily interpreted. However, to many at the time, it seemed as if the rule of the Saints for a thousand years was at hand. So they read the signs of the times. Among a people of the Book, as it almost seemed the English had become, such scriptures enhanced the excitement and the expectation. In 1641, a Puritan pamphleteer called Hanser Knollys interpreted the events of that year as foreshadowing the imminence of the Millennium:

Though the governors of Judah (ie., Charles and his ministers) *have counted them factious and schismatics and Puritans, there is a time coming when the governors of Judah shall be convinced of the excellency of God's people, so convinced as to say in their hearts that the inhabitants of Jerusalem, that is, the Saints of God gathered together in a church, are the best commonwealth's men: not seditious men, not factious, not disturbers of the state . . . This shall be when the Lord God Omnipotent reigneth in his Church. And through God's mercy we see light peeping out this way.*[7]

This was 1641, the year when Strafford was executed and Laud imprisoned in the Tower. It was the year when the Commons passed the Grand Remonstrance. The light indeed was 'peeping out this way'. In this same year Milton wrote a pamphlet account of the Reformation. It ends with a remarkable passage which shows Milton in a state of exaltation. It also shows his passionate desire that his should be the voice to record and celebrate these wonderful events. He, too, is looking to the day of the Lord and the reign of the Saints:

Then amidst the Hymns and Hallelujahs of Saints some one may perhaps be heard offering at high strains in new and lofty Measures to sing and celebrate thy divine Mercies, and marvellous Judgements in this Land throughout all Ages; whereby this great and Warlike Nation instructed and inured to the fervent and continual practice of Truth and

11. *The Day of Wrath* by Dürer from the Apocalypse series, 1498, illustrates the Second Coming of Christ on the Day of Wrath (see Rev. 6:15–16)

And the kings of the earth, and the great men, and the rich men, and the chief captains, and the mighty men, and every bond-man, and every freeman, hid themselves in the dens and in the rocks of the mountains; And said to the mountains and rocks, Fall on us, and hide us from the face of him that sitteth on the throne, and from the wrath of the Lamb.

(The Mansell Collection)

> *Righteousness, and casting far from her the rages of her old vices, may press on hard to that high and happy emulation to be found the soberest, wisest and most Christian People at that day when thou the Eternal and* shortly-expected (my emphasis) *King shalt open the Clouds to judge the several Kingdoms of the World, and distributing National Honours and Rewards to Religious and just Commonwealths, shalt put an end to all Earthly Tyrannies, proclaiming thy universal mild Monarchy through Heaven and Earth. Where they undoubtedly that by their Labours, Counsels and Prayers have been earnest for the Common good of Religion and their Country, shall receive, above the inferior Orders of the Blessed, the Regal addition of Principalities, Legions, and Thrones into their glorious Titles, and in supereminence of beatific Vision progressing the dateless and irrevoluble Circle of Eternity shall clasp inseparable Hands with joy, and bliss in over-measure for ever.*[8]

It was an ecstatic moment, however brief, and is a measure of the tragedy of disappointment.

WORK FOR THE COMMONWEALTH

Milton was able to do little during the time of fighting. At his Aldersgate home, he was teaching his nephews and various other pupils. In 1643 he married and the same year his wife left him. Instead of political writings, his pamphleteering was now in favour of divorce, another aspect of freedom, perhaps!

There was always a possibility of active service; at one time Royalist forces were beyond Reading. Milton believed in taking physical exercise, as he said in one of his pamphlets against episcopacy:

> *with useful and generous labours preserving the body's health and hardiness to render lightsome, clear, and not lumpish obedience to the mind, to the cause of religion, and our country's liberty, when it shall require firm hearts in sound bodies to stand and cover their stations, rather than to see the ruin of our protestation and the inforcement of a slavish life.*[9]

It was not really until the execution of the King in January 1649, that he was able to deploy his talents in the direct service of the Commonwealth.

The country was very seriously divided over the trial and execution of their King. The Parliamentary forces had been supported by the active minority of the people; probably the majority of the nation was unwilling to see such extreme measures taken against the monarchy. It was a decision of the army and a consequence of what seemed to them Charles' persistent bad faith in negotiations. But it was difficult to justify and the reaction across the Channel in Europe was one of horror. History knew many usurpers but there was no precedent for a parliament trying and beheading a king. The government badly needed its case put well.

They were thus very pleased by the support of Milton. First of all, he wrote *Tenure of Kings and Magistrates*, published a month after the execution. It begins:

> *If men within themselves would be governed by reason, and not generally give up their understanding to a double tyranny, of Custom from without, and blind affections within, they would discern better, what it is to favour and uphold the Tyrant of a Nation.*[10]

Note Milton's continued emphasis upon reason—the full exercise of all our God-given faculties.

In this pamphlet he stated, with some moderation, the case for removing Charles:

> *Since the king or magistrate holds his authority of the people, both originally and naturally, for their good in the first place, and not his own, then may the people, as oft as they shall judge it for the best, either choose him or reject him, retain him or depose him though no tyrant, merely by the liberty and right of freeborn men to be governed as seems to them best.*[10]

This is a revolutionary doctrine. It fits well with what we have already learned about Milton's attitude to freedom. But it was by no means the common view of the time. The logic of the argument had put Milton well over to what today we might term the left in politics.

However, for Milton, the direct consequence of his writing was a government appointment in March 1649, as Secretary for Foreign Tongues to the Council of State. In effect, he had two jobs. He was to assist the Council (this meant Cromwell) in correspondence with foreign governments. Milton was the finest writer in Latin of his day. He was also virtually the official apologist for the Government. Ironically, he was also responsible for the licensing of publications. As a censor, he was generous.

The pamphleteering was largely in order to cope with royalist argument and invective. *Eikonoclastes*, for example, was an attack on a book which used notes left by the king and treated him as a martyr for the Anglican faith. He also wrote two essays in Latin against the French scholar Claude de Saumaise (Salmasius) who had been engaged by Charles II. The second of these was very much in praise of Cromwell. There is no doubt of Milton's pride and pleasure in this writing. In Latin he had a European audience. He was the spokesman for his country and his cause. In itself this was an epic task. His vision of himself was perhaps rather inflated, certainly in this from the *Defensio Secunda pro Populo Anglicano*:

> *Surrounded by congregated multitudes, I now imagine that, from the columns of Hercules to the Indian Ocean, I behold the nations of the earth recovering that liberty which they so long had lost, and that the people of this island are transporting to other countries a plant of more beneficial qualities, and more noble growth, than that which Triptolemus is reported to have carried from region to region; that they are disseminating the blessings of civilisation and freedom among cities, kingdoms, and nations.*[11]

It is not uncommon for revolutionaries to want to export their revolutions. This pamphlet was written, though, at a bad time. It was in 1654 just after he finally lost his sight, and he was unwell.

By 1655, he seems to have fully recovered in health. It appears too that this was a period in which he was engaged on major projects. One was *Paradise Lost*, a second was *The History of Britain* ('*collected out of the antietest and best authors*'). This was published in 1670. A third was the vast labour of *De Doctrina Christiana*. Although written during the period 1655–60, this was never published in his lifetime, but it came out first in two volumes as late as 1825.

THE RESTORATION

On the very eve of the Restoration, in 1660, Milton wrote *The Ready and Easy Way to Establish a Free Commonwealth*. It was a last attempt to persuade his fellow countrymen by reason not to give hostage to a reactionary Fortune, '*to stay these ruinous proceedings*'. He could not see why men, tired of civil strife, longed for the quietude of a restored monarchy. To him, reason dictated that England should:

> *have our forces by sea and land, either of a faithful Army or a settled Militia, in our hands to the firm establishing of a free Commonwealth, public accounts under our own inspection, general laws and taxes with their causes in our domestic suffrages, judicial laws, offices and ornaments at home in our own ordering and administration, all distinction of lords and commoners, that may any way divide or sever the public interest, removed.*[12]

Arguably, the programme is not yet completed.

The political experience was very relevant to the writing of the last great poems. All three involve *debate.* At one level, Milton could describe some of Satan's party:

> *Others apart sat on a Hill retir'd,*
> *In thoughts more elevate, and reasond high*
> *Of Providence, Foreknowledge, Will and Fate,*
> *Fixt Fate, free Will, Foreknowledge absolute,*
> *And found no end, in wandring mazes lost.*[13]

This is not a bad account of the Westminster Assembly of Presbyterian divines which sought to make England of that church. At a deeper level, the poems are full of Milton's concern with free will and with issues of freedom and tyranny. The bitter disappointment of the Restoration drove Milton, blind as he was, from public life. He remained true to his self-dedication. What he said in 1660, he could have spoken on his death bed in 1674: '*What I have spoken, is the language of that which is not called amiss "the Good Old Cause".*'

[1] *Instrument of Government* (1653) [2] Milton *Reason of Church Government* (1642) [3] Milton *De Doctrina Christiana* (*circa* 1655–60) [4] Milton *Paradise Lost* XII, 83–96 [5] Milton *Areopagitica* (1644) [6] Revelation 20 vv. 1–5 [7] Hanser Knolly's *A Glimpse of Sion's Glory* (1641) [8] Milton *Of Reformation Touching Church Discipline in England* (1641) [9] Milton *Apology for Smectymnuus* (1642) [10] Milton *Tenure of Kings and Magistrates* (1649) [11] Milton *Defensio Secunda pro Populo Anglicano* (1654) [12] Milton *The Ready and Easy Way to Establish a Free Commonwealth* (1660) [13] *Paradise Lost* II, 557–61

4

Milton and Europe

It was in the spring of 1638 that Milton set off on his European tour. Such a tour was an accepted way of completing the education of a gentleman. But it was as a scholar that John Milton went. By this stage, he had already written a number of poems and the masque *Comus* had been performed. He wrote to a number of people in Europe. He set off on his travels, too, with some useful letters of introduction.

It was a very important journey for him. He was to visit Italy, the birthplace of the classics and the home of art and scholarship. In the seventeenth century, in spite of Elizabeth, the Armada victory and the great seamen who crossed the oceans of the world, England was a small country on the edge of Europe. There were no colonies to make the English feel themselves at the centre of the world. Knowledge, be it of science or the arts, seemed to flow out from Italy and reach these islands at the last.

Milton knew he was to become a great writer, the poet of his nation. As we shall see (Chapter 6) he was busy on a long preparation for the task. It was of the utmost importance to him to spend time in Italy for three main reasons.

1 It was the land of Virgil. Under the Roman sky, he could absorb the true atmosphere of the Latin genius.

2 In Italy, he could meet scholars, see great modern art and listen to music. He would be closely in touch with a European culture that was anything but provincial.

3 He could himself become a member of that larger European community. To a writer like Milton, who found little in the literature of his day in Britain to meet his needs and ambitions, Italy was an oasis.

There was a short stay first in Paris; he was not very impressed. Then he hurried south and over the border beyond Nice to Genoa. He spent time in Florence and Rome. He visited Venice and Naples. Everywhere he was treated with respect—a scholar among fellow scholars. At home he had, as yet, little reputation. In Italy he was one of a European fellowship of men of letters. His high opinion of himself was confirmed, and, therefore, the visit was an unqualified success.

But what were the lasting results? As we shall see, Milton's own poetic writing was so unfashionable and individual that it is hard to pin down influences of any kind. Certainly, his European contacts helped him to get the job of defending in writing the execution of the King. His direct knowledge of the continent was no doubt helpful to him as Latin Secretary.

Remember, too, that Milton wrote as fluently in Latin as in English. He knew Italian but Latin was the language of both diplomatic and scholarly discussion. He wrote letters to his Italian friends in Latin. In the seventeenth century it was by no means a dead language. Everyone comments on the Latin features of the style of *Paradise Lost*. In a way, he was being more European than his fellow English writers.

There are a few more positive influences of the trip. Firstly, Milton wanted to write an epic poem—the epic poem in English. There were no epics in English. Spenser's *Faerie Queene* was the nearest but everyone agreed that whatever it was, it was not an epic—like Virgil's *Aeneid* for example. But there was an epic tradition in Italy. In Naples, he met John Baptista Manso, a rich and elderly nobleman. Manso had been the patron of Torquato Tasso. That is, he had recognized the literary genius of Tasso and had supported him so that he might write. Such patronage was felt by many noblemen to be a duty. Tasso was an epic poet in the classical tradition. The contact with Manso was emotionally very important to Milton.

12. St Peter's in Rome, designed by Bellini (1598–1680), showing the Piazza San Pietro (The Mansell Collection)

Secondly, he was, in general, brought much more closely in touch with European art and music. When he became blind, he became dependent on his visual memory. We must remember that the great poems were all written after he lost his sight. The great dome of St Peter's in Rome (Fig. 12) was by Michelangelo, and Milton retained a picture of it in his mind.

Consider this passage from *Paradise Lost* where Satan and his hosts are cast out of heaven and landed by the shore of the infernal lake. There the fallen angels built their capital of Pandemonium:

> *Anon out of the earth a Fabrick huge*
> *Rose like an Exhalation, with the sound*
> *Of Dulcet Symphonies and voices sweet:*
> *Built like a Temple, where* Pilasters *round*
> *Were set, and Doric pillars overlaid*
> *With Gold'n Architrave; nor did there want*
> *Cornice or Freeze, with bossy Sculptures grav'n;*
> *The Roof was fretted Gold.*[1]

This is no piece of domestic Gothic. This is the *Baroque* architecture that Milton found in Italy.

The painting (Fig. 13) by the French painter, Nicholas Poussin (1594–1665), is a characteristic work of seventeenth-century art

13. *A Dance to the Music of Time* by Nicholas Poussin (Reproduced by permission of the Trustees of the Wallace Collection, London)

which shows the ideas of landscape at that period. It is a pastoral scene of natural landscape but the figures are classical—gods and goddesses of ancient Greece, whom we recognize as we have read about them in books. There will be a deeper meaning, usually religious. Apollo in this picture is shown as God of the Sun. But he is also ruler of Time and God of poetry. The world dances to the music of time and the heavens.

Compare the Poussin *Landscape with a Snake* (Fig. 14) with this extract from *Paradise Lost*. Satan sees Paradise for the first time:

So on he fares, and to the border comes
Of Eden, *where delicious Paradise,*
Now nearer, Crowns with her enclosure green,
As with a rural mound the champain head
Of a steep wilderness, whose hairie sides
With thicket overgrown, grottesque and wilde,
Access deni'd; and over head up grew
Insuperable highth of loftiest shade,
Cedar, and Pine, and Firr, and branching Palm,
A Silvan Scene, and as the ranks ascend
Shade above shade, a woodie Theatre
Of stateliest view.[2]

We do not see landscape today in this orderly and artful manner. We see nature as our eyes have been trained to see it through modern paintings and camera angles which, themselves, reflect our attitudes. Milton 'saw' nature with much the same eye as the European artists of his time—reflecting the handiwork of God and Man.

14. *Landscape with a Snake* by Nicholas Poussin (Reproduced by courtesy of the Trustees, The National Gallery, London)

A third influence is less directly obvious—more a matter of viewpoint.

Look again at the photograph of the piazza outside St Peter's in Rome (Fig. 12). The approach to the cathedral was designed by Gianlorenzo Bernini (1598–1680). Milton almost certainly met him in Rome. Bernini's original design has been somewhat ruined this century by Mussolini who was responsible for the wide avenue which now leads into the piazza. As a result, a visitor to Rome can see from far back the cathedral and something of the space before it. The original intention was one of surprise. The pilgrim would find his way through the narrow and crowded streets of Rome and suddenly break into the piazza and the space and power of its architecture.

In a similar way, Satan, after a flight of terrible difficulties, at last reaches the Earth, newly created, of which he has only heard:

Looks down with wonder at the sudden view
Of all this World at once. As when a Scout
Through dark and desart wayes with peril gone
All night; at last by break of chearful dawne
Obtains the brow of some high-climbing Hill,
Which to his eye discovers unaware
The goodly prospect of some forren land
First-seen, or some renownd Metropolis
With glistering Spires and Pinnacles adornd,
Which now the Rising Sun guilds with his beams.[3]

This shows surprise and power. In his architecture Bernini *asserts* the authority of the Roman church. In *Paradise Lost* Milton *asserts* the power of God.

In the Bernini statue of *Apollo and Daphne* (Fig. 26). Bernini has caught a moment of change, of metamorphosis. Daphne is changing with terrifying rapidity into an olive tree so that, escaping, she is already imprisoned—rooted to the earth, limbs becoming branches and body the trunk. There are central moments in Milton where we also witness transformations. In this one, Satan returns to Hell in triumph for his victory in tempting Eve.

a while he stood, expecting
Thir universal shout and high applause
To fill his eare, when contrary he hears
On all sides, from innumerable tongues
A dismal universal hiss, the sound

Of public scorn; he wonderd but not long
Had leasure, wondring at himself now more;
His Visage drawn he felt to sharp and spare,
His Armes clung to his Ribs, his Leggs entwining
Each other, till supplanted down he fell
A monstrous Serpent on his Belly prone,
Reluctant, but in vaine: a greater power
Now rul'd him, punisht in the shape he sinnd,
According to his doom.[4]

Fourthly, when he was in Venice, he shipped home a chest of purchases, not art, but music. His father, as we have noticed, was a musician of considerable skill. Milton himself was deeply concerned with music; it was an important part of his life. As you read his poetry, look out for sound effects and references to music. After all, in *Comus* he had already written words to be set to music. The organist at St Mark's in Venice at the time of Milton's visit was Monteverdi, one of the first and one of the greatest of opera composers. Milton himself thought music was the handmaiden of poetry. Its main rôle was to make poetry more effective—at a different level—a not wholly unfamiliar view today. So he was very interested in Monteverdi's 'drama for music'.

A fifth influence was his visit to the old and blind Galileo. To Milton Galileo was a symbol of all that was wrong with Papacy—the stifling of Reason by bigotry. Whether Milton looked through Galileo's telescope, we do not know. He certainly refers to it (*Paradise Lost* V, 261–3). He also has Satan's landing on the surface of the sun appear as a sun spot. Galileo first noted the presence of spots on the sun, a discovery greeted with horror by all those who believed in the perfection of heavenly bodies.

[1] *Paradise Lost* I, 710–17 [2] *ibid.* IV, 131–43 [3] *ibid.* III, 542–51
[4] *ibid.* X, 504–17

5

The Milton Universe

In what they write, both the novelist and the poet show a geography of their minds. The landscape of the story or the poem is created out of all kinds of experience. Probably most of us think that this is largely the experience of living. Indeed, in this century, we value direct experience quite highly. But this is a very limited world for much experience only touches us on the surface. The poet writes both from the surface and from the depths.

Many of the deep experiences in Milton's life were in books. The world of Homer and of Virgil, which he had so intensively explored in his education, was alive and present to him. *Their* poetry, their islands and their sea, their gods and their heroes were constantly present in Milton's mind. Classical comparisons came *naturally* to his mind. There was more to it than that. The writers of Greece and Rome were a major part of Milton's knowledge and understanding of the world. It was a tradition of knowledge and thinking that was alive in Milton and his contemporaries. Galileo, the modern scientist, was a man like Socrates. He suffered, and Socrates died, for truth and reason.

Co-existing in Milton's mind with this deeply-felt knowledge of the classical world was the Bible. In classical writing could be found the wisdom of *men*; in the Bible was the wisdom of *God*. Whatever Milton questioned in the orthodoxies of his day (and he was very bold in questioning), he never questioned the Bible. To him, and to nearly everyone in his day, the Bible was true in every line for every line was the Word of God. The Bible was not easy to understand. It often spoke in riddles. A man had to *work* at his Bible, if he were to understand what God had to say. There had to be constant study and prayer if the message was to speak loudly and clearly. It was also true that the Bible had been written in past times. God had spoken to the limited understandings of those times. So, for example, the story of Adam and Eve and the Fall was literally true, taught us about the nature of God and man's relationship to God, and was also written to suit the minds of people many centuries before. Modern knowledge *must* be used to illumine ancient truth.

John Milton lived in a period when our knowledge of the world was expanding rapidly. His education had been a Renaissance one. Remember that the study of the classics had seemed to men of the Renaissance a liberating force. Greek science and philosophy studied afresh swept away medieval cobwebs. Yet older ways of looking at the world remained. In Milton's day, the new science had not yet become taken for granted. Most educated people, for example, accepted the roundness of the earth. Many remained uncertain whether the earth circled the sun or was properly at the centre of a universe which wheeled around the earth. In any case, John Milton had only a layman's interest in science. It was interesting at times but not important in the same way as other forms of knowledge.

However, science could be grist to the poetic mill. So could any knowledge. For Milton's poetic ambitions, an almost encyclopedic knowledge was essential. So we find him using, in the great poems, ideas from all ages. As both old and new views of the world were available to him, he could use either or both where it suited. Remember, though, that he could not use the Bible in this way. That was given. Other knowledge served only to illumine the central truths.

Most of the examples that follow are taken from *Paradise Lost*. It is in this poem that Milton needed the greatest range of ideas. He had to describe the whole universe—heaven, hell, sun, moon, planets, stars and earth—and make the cosmography as convincing and as coherent as possible.

MODERN TECHNOLOGY AND SCIENCE

Although Milton did not take part directly in the Civil War—he did a little military training in case the Royalists reached London—he was well aware of what war meant. The area between Oxford and London was much fought over. He ascribed the invention of gunpowder and the cannon to Satan. The 'science' of war is the only science he condemns.

Satan uses his newly-invented cannon against the angelic army of Christ during the war in heaven. The effects were appalling:

Immediate in a flame,
But soon obscur'd with smoak, all Heav'n appeerd,
From those deep-throated Engins belcht, whose roar
Emboweld with outragious noise the Air,

And all her entrails tore, disgorging foule
Thir devilish glut, chaind Thunderbolts and Hail
Of Iron Globes, which on the Victor Host
Leveld, with such impetuous furie smote,
That whom they hit, none on thir feet might stand,
Though standing else as Rocks, but down they fell
By thousands, Angel on Arch-Angel rowld,
The sooner for thir Arms.[1]

We have already noted Milton's concern for Galileo. At University he had advocated the 'new learning'—the rather more scientific approach of Francis Bacon to knowledge. He was clearly fascinated by the telescope. For example, he compares Raphael's remarkably clear view of the earth from a distance with the effect of looking through a telescope (*Paradise Lost* V, 257–63). However, he was much less clear about microscopes—he seems to have thought they were some kind of magic X-ray eye.

He was, of course, not a scientist. He was not interested in that kind of truth. So he had no qualms in using old and new ideas about the earth as it suited him. When the sun sets, we can either think traditionally of its passage across the heavens or we can be up to date and think of the earth turning on her axis. Take your pick:

whether the prime Orb,
Incredible how swift, had thither rowld
Diurnal, or this less volubil Earth
By shorter flight to th'East, had left him there
Arraying with reflected Purple and Gold
The Clouds that on his Western Throne attend.[2]

There were two main ways of explaining the apparent movement of heavenly bodies still current in the seventeenth century. The older was the Ptolemaic (Fig. 15). The assumption here was that the earth was still and at the centre of the Universe. Sun, moon, stars and planets circled round the earth in a daily pattern. The problem, of course, was to explain the observable movements of the planets. The Ptolemaic system provided a complicated mathematical explanation. Round the earth was a series of translucent spheres in which were placed in sequence the various heavenly bodies. The spheres were themselves controlled by the final sphere, that of Heaven where God and His Angels dwelt. What we see on earth at the centre is the movement of these spheres in which the heavenly bodies are placed.

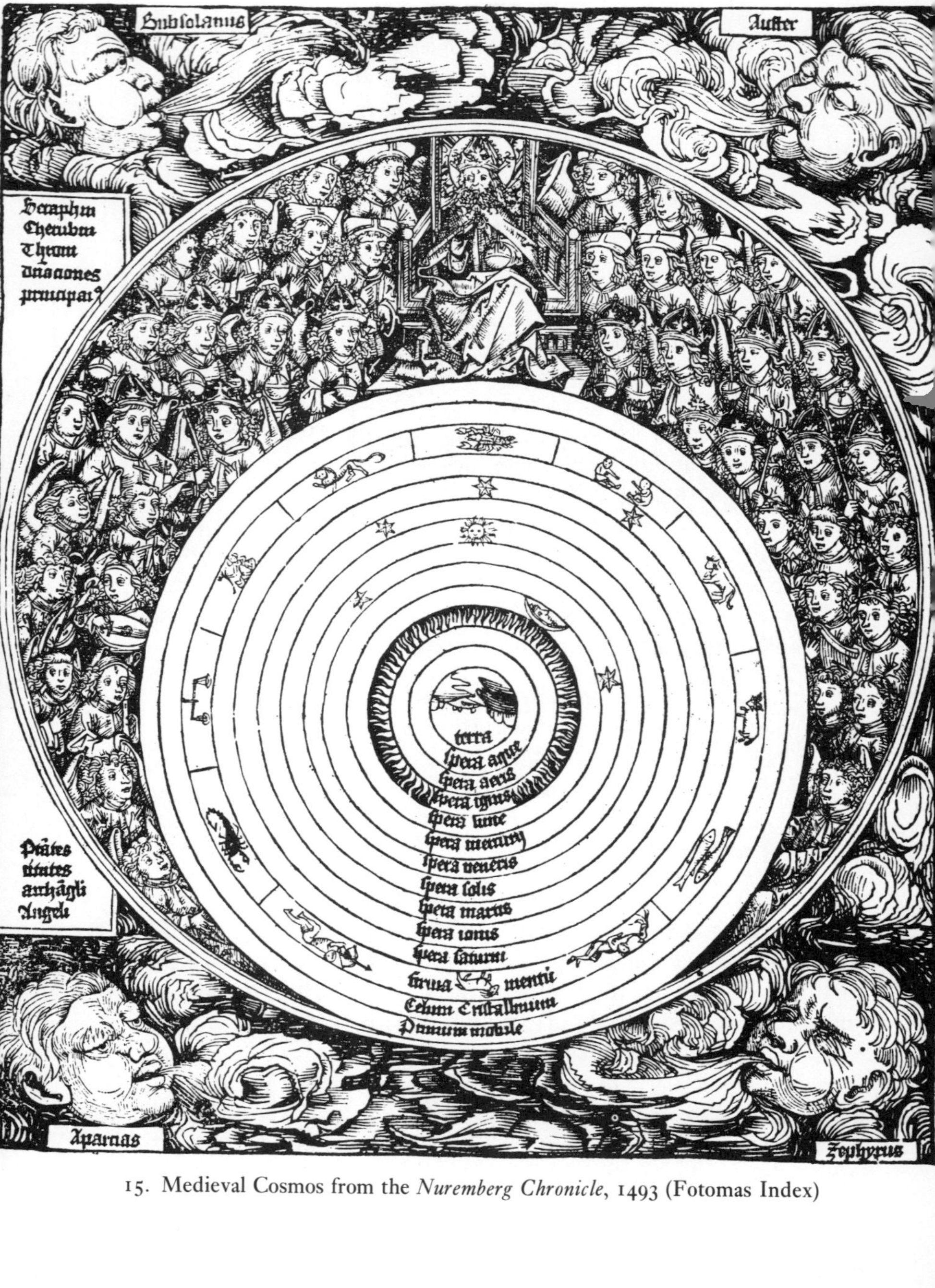

15. Medieval Cosmos from the *Nuremberg Chronicle*, 1493 (Fotomas Index)

At the time, it was a difficult theory to attack. After all, it provided an explanation for commonsense observation. The Bible assumes that the earth is at the centre of the universe, and so did Aristotle. Men felt they were at the centre of creation.

There was another important feature of this belief which was linked to the biblical notion of the Fall. Above the moon, all was fixed and eternal; there was no change or decay. Only below the sphere of the moon was there change and death.

The alternative was the theory of Copernicus (1473–1543). This placed the sun at the centre of the Universe. Earth and the planets moved around the sun. The mathematics of the theory were much simpler but it was not easy for ordinary people to accept. After all, it took man from his position at the centre; the earth was just another planet. By Milton's time, the Copernican theory had gained ground among the educated. By the Restoration, after which *Paradise Lost* was written, it became scientific orthodoxy.

Milton himself found the Copernican theory the rational one. It was not, however, a great deal of use to him in *Paradise Lost*. The discoveries of astronomy helped to create a sense of the vastness of the universe: In Book VIII, Adam comments:

> *When I behold this goodly Frame, this World*
> *Of Heav'n and Earth consisting, and compute*
> *Thir magnitudes, this Earth a spot, a graine,*
> *An Atom, with the Firmament compar'd*
> *And all her numberd Starrs that seem to rowle*
> *Spaces incomprehensible.*[3]

He asks Raphael for an explanation. The answer seems to suggest that God had deliberately hidden the details of the universal mechanism. Men had better things to do than ask questions about the heavens.

In fact, Milton had a clear interest in some degree of vagueness. After all, in *Paradise Lost* he was committed to scenes in both Heaven and Hell and on the Earth. It was vital to convey a sense of immensity. Satan's journey from Hell to Earth took him across vast distances of space. The cosmography had to be plausible; it also had to reflect the 'message' as it were. For the purposes of the poem it was best to imagine the earth as being at the centre of the created universe.

He was also writing about the Earth before the Fall. After all, after that catastrophic event, the universe could well have taken its modern form. So Satan walks on the outer shell of the universe. He sees the whole arrangement of spheres hanging from heaven on a golden chain. His journey is from a remote Inferno towards the centre, for man is at the heart of God's plans for creation. Before the Fall, the Earth is a perfect sphere. It is not surprising that Satan against the sun looks like a sunspot—a sign of imperfection. Satan's shield looks like the moon today—spotted. These are marks of sin and decay.

The climate of Paradise is, of course, perfect. There were no seasons. After the Fall, there were tremendous changes. Life became seasonal—summer giving way to winter and death and thence to the fresh life of spring in turn to die. For the explanation of the change, Milton suggests two ideas:

Some say he bid his Angels turne ascanse
The Poles of Earth twice ten degrees and more
From the Suns Axle; they with labour pushd
Oblique the Centric Globe: Som say the Sun
Was bid turn Reines from th'Equinoctial Rode.[4]

First he gives us the modern, then the ancient account.

ASTROLOGY

Milton, unlike very many of his contemporaries, seemed to have little belief in the influence of the stars and planets on our lives—though he did once have his horoscope cast. To him, the world was basically rational, as must be the creation of God. Astrology in any case seemed to deny Free Will:

Let no man seek
Henceforth to be foretold what shall befall
Him or his Children, evil he may be sure,
Which neither his foreknowing can prevent,
And hee the future evil shall no less
In apprehension then in substance feel
Grievous to bear.[5]

But do not be surprised to find Milton, on occasion, making *use* of astrological concepts. Strange happenings in heaven were popularly thought to presage disaster. As imagery, astrology could provide a particular emotional effect. After all, Milton did not believe in the gods and goddesses of ancient Greece. Their legends gave body to Christian doctrines; the classical mythology was a source of valuable illustrations.

THE CHAIN OF BEING

One of the most profound concepts of the Middle Ages was that of the Chain of Being. There is a natural order or *hierarchy* for everything in creation. Everything has its place from the lowest to the highest.

> *In the universal order of things the top of an inferior class touches the bottom of a superior; as for instance oysters, which, occupying as it were the lowest position in the class of animals, scarcely rise above the life of plants, because they cling to the earth without motion and possess the sense of touch alone. The upper surface of the earth is in contact with the lower surface of water; the highest part of the waters touchest the lowest part of the air, and so by a ladder of ascent to the outermost sphere of the universe.*[6]

Everything, then, has a place in this order. In the earth, man himself has the supremacy but beyond him the chain of being ascends through the orders of the heavenly bodies, the orders of the angels up to God himself from whom the chain descends. So no part of the universe was superfluous; everything had a part to play. This gave a dignity even to the lowest in creation. There is too a fullness in creation. Though there is death, there is birth. Spenser wrote this about the Garden of Adonis:

> *Daily they grow and daily forth are sent*
> *Into the world it to replenish more;*
> *Yet is the stock not lessened nor spent*
> *But still remains in everlasting store,*
> *As it at first created was of yore.*[7]

God sent Raphael to Paradise and the newly-created Adam to teach him. After a meal (Milton's angels, though of a more 'spiritual' substance than man, still ate and drank and, apparently, made love), Raphael, named as the 'great Hierarch' begins to explain to Adam and Eve the order of creation. In this long quotation, notice how God is the source of life, how all creation has its degree and how, even, within man, each part has its place moving upwards to the soul.

> *O* Adam, *one Almightie is, from whom*
> *All things proceed, and up to him return,*
> *If not deprav'd from good, created all*

Such to perfection, one first matter all,
Indu'd with various forms, various degrees
Of substance, and in things that live, of life;
But more refin'd, more spiritous and pure,
As neerer to him plac't or neerer tending
Each in thir several active Spheárs assignd,
Till body up to spirit work, in bounds
Proportiond to each kind. So from the root
Springs lighter the green stalk, from thence the leaves
More aerie, last the bright consummat floure
Spirits odorous breathes: flours and thir fruit
Mans nourishment, by gradual scale sublim'd
To vital spirits aspire, to animal,
To intellectual, give both life and sense,
Fansie and understanding, whence the Soule
Reason receives, and reason is her being.[8]

Notice the ascent is from the more material to the less. Notice also that Raphael speaks of creation aspiring all the time to the more spiritual. All things proceed from God. They return to him—unless they have been corrupted by evil. They then fall towards Hell.

The view is a comprehensive one. The great hierarchies have the poetic splendour of a mighty procession.

MAN

In Book II of *Paradise Lost*, Milton describes Satan escaping through Hellgate and setting off on his long and arduous flight to Earth. Satan passes through the region of Chaos—primeval matter not yet ordered as new worlds. The whole description is a curious and typical mixture of old and new. However, behind much of this passage is another medieval concept—a kind of atomic theory:

Before thir eyes in sudden view appear
The secrets of the hoarie Deep, a dark
Illimitable Ocean without bound,
Without dimension, where length, bredth and highth,
And time and place are lost; where eldest Night
And Chaos, *Ancestors of Nature, hold*
Eternal Anarchie, amidst the noise
Of endless warrs, and by confusion stand.

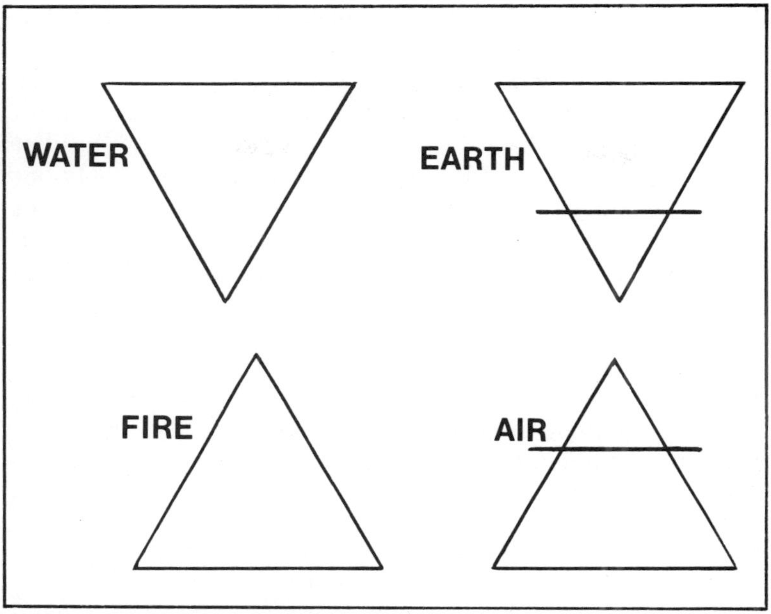

16. The alchemical symbols for the elements

For hot, cold, moist and dry, four Champions fierce
Strive here for Maistrie, and to Battel bring
Thir embryon Atoms.[9]

There are four elements—earth, water, air and fire. These elements had the primary qualities of dry, moist, cold and hot. So earth is cold and dry; water is cold and moist; air is hot and moist; fire is hot and dry.

All matter is composed of one or more of these elements, including man. Man is, of course, the *link* between earth and heaven. If we think of the universe as the macrocosm, then man is the microcosm. In himself, he shows all the elements and hierarchies of the universe in miniature—in microcosm. So man is made of four elements or *humours*: there is *melancholy* like earth, cold and dry; there is *phlegm* like water, cold and moist; there is *blood* like air, hot and moist, and there is *choler* like fire, hot and dry. The fortunate man was he who had a proper balance in his make-up of all four humours. Excess of one or the other produced the various temperaments—the sanguine (blood), phlegmatic, choleric and melancholic. Illness was an excess that needed correcting. Blood-letting, for example, by removing blood would restore the correct balance. A man with a fever clearly had an excess of hot and moist!

Man had body and soul. These were linked by 'spirit'. Rather as water boils to form first steam and then an invisible gas, so the humours (in the liver, in fact) turned into 'spirit' which rose to the brain and there nourished the rational soul. Hence the phrase still in use today—to be 'out of spirits'. Body and soul were thus not actually separate. Or so Milton felt quite strongly. He could not believe in a soul that could, for example, leave one body at death and take residence in a new-born baby. Nor did he believe in a soul that is ghost at death or goes to some heaven or hell. Death was death for both body and soul until the final resurrection. This was not, by the way, particularly orthodox as a belief but, then, Milton never was a conformist. He was, however, a great believer in *temperance*—that is, in having the right balance of food and drink. This followed from the notion of temperaments, of course. So, when Satan tempted Eve, he endeavoured to interfere with the balance of her temperament:

Squat like a Toad, close at the eare of Eve*;*
Assaying by his Devilish art to reach
The Organs of her Fancie, and with them forge
Illusions as he lists, Fantasms and Dreams;
Or if, inspiring venom, he might taint
Th'animal spirits that from pure blood arise
Like gentle breaths from Rivers pure, thence raise
At least distemperd, discontented thoughts,
Vain hopes, vain aimes, inordinate desires
Blown up with high conceits ingendring pride.[10]

THE MUSIC OF THE SPHERES

As we have seen, Milton drew from contemporary science and from Elizabethan conceptions of the nature of the world as suited his grand scheme. Without doubt, there were elements in the older view of the world that appealed profoundly to the poet in Milton. The early biographer, Jonathan Richardson, who knew people who knew Milton, wrote (in 1734):

Music he loved extremely, and understood well. 'Tis said he composed, though nothing of that has been brought down to us. He diverted himself with performing, which they say he did well on the organ and bass viol; and this was a great relief to him after he had lost his sight.[11]

Milton speaks in 'Il Penseroso' of the cathedral:

There let the pealing Organ blow,
To the full voic'd Choir below,
In Service high, and Anthems cleer,
As may with sweetnes, through mine ear,
Dissolve me into extasies,
And bring all Heav'n before mine eyes.[12]

The Greek mathematician and mystic, Pythagoras, first noted the connection between musical intervals and proportions expressed mathematically. This led, in due course, to the belief that the whole order of the universe would be found to be mathematically based. For example, the relationship between the spheres of sun, planets and fixed stars could be expressed mathematically. If mathematically, then musically. The spheres must be in *harmony*. Each sphere has its own note and together they make the music of the spheres. The whole is governed by the celestial sphere, the *primum mobile* or prime mover, which is, as it were, the conductor of the heavenly orchestra. Look at the drawing of the medieval cosmos (Fig. 15). The earth is surrounded by zones corresponding to the four elements. Then come the planetary spheres—moon, Mercury, Venus, Sun, Mars, Jupiter, Saturn, the fixed stars, or the celestial or crystal sphere turned by the *primum mobile*—eight spheres corresponding to the octave.

Milton naturally found this concept attractive. In *Arcades*, written in his early twenties, we find:

But els in deep of night when drowsines
Hath lockt up mortal sense, then listen I
To the celestial Sirens harmony,
That sit upon the nine enfolded Spheres.[13]

So, in *Paradise Lost*, Milton speaks of music in heaven:

That day, as other solem dayes, they spent
In song and dance about the sacred Hill,
Mystical dance, which yonder starrie Spheare
Of Planets and of fixt in all her Wheeles
Resembles nearest, mazes intricate,
Eccentric, intervolv'd, yet regular
Then most, when most irregular they seem:
And in thir motions harmonie Divine
So smooths her charming tones, that Gods own ear
List'ns delighted.[14]

John Dryden was the great poet of the Restoration. It was his critical acclaim that did much to bring readers to Milton, otherwise an unpopular survivor of Cromwellian days, a man out of tune with a worldly and conservative period. Dryden in a song on the day of the patron saint of music, St Cecilia, last gave full expression to the harmony of creation. The lines are in accord with Milton:

From Harmony, from heavenly Harmony
This universal frame began;
When Nature underneath a heap
Of Jarring Atomes lay,
And could not heave her Head,
The tuneful Voice was heard from high,
Arise, ye more than dead.
Then cold and hot and moist and dry
In order to their stations leap,
And MUSICK'S pow'r obey.
From Harmony, from heavenly Harmony
This universal Frame began:
From Harmony to Harmony
Through all the Compass of the Notes it ran,
The Diapason closing full in Man.[15]

No wonder there was also music in Paradise (*Paradise Lost* IV, 677).

REASON

But God left free the will, for what obeys
Reason, is free, and Reason he made right.[16]

So said Adam to Eve. We live in a period in which we are only too conscious of the fallibility or, perhaps, the limits of human reason. We are aware of depths in ourselves below the level of consciousness. Some of us are thus inclined to trust more to feeling, to emotion, than to the rational. Mistakenly, we equate the rational with that dangerous selfishness that builds a seemingly scientific house upon the sands of passion and prejudice.

To Milton, Reason was the law of God. He believed

> *that there is a godlike principle in Man, and that that principle is to be found in the Reason or Understanding, and the Will. Whatever feeds the Understanding therefore, and procures true knowledge and wisdom, is for him of the highest value; hence the importance of study and education.*[17]

Remember that what is good moves upward towards God; what is corrupt moves downwards. In Man is a tug of war between Reason and Passion—the upward moving and the downward. Only if Reason and Passion work together can man be happy. A happy man is one whose desires do not clash with his moral sense. As God must, by definition, be the fount of Reason, so to obey God or to seek to understand and follow the will of God, is to act most closely in accord with reason. Men have dreams, even 'wicked' dreams; they are beset with powerful emotions. All is well, including the emotions, if they are under the rule of Reason.

To complete the circle, Reason is therefore that which is in harmony, that which operates to maintain or restore a proper balance or order. By disobedience to God and eating of the forbidden apple, Adam and Eve let disorder and disharmony into our world, for they are the offspring of sin.

[1] *Paradise Lost* VI, 584–95 [2] *ibid.* IV, 592–7 [3] *ibid.* VIII, 15–20 [4] *ibid.* X, 668–72 [5] *ibid.* XI, 770–76 [6] Ranulph Higden *Polychronicon* (*circa* 1352) [7] Spenser *Faerie Queene* Book 3 Canto VI Stanza 36 [8] *Paradise Lost* V, 469–87 [9] *ibid.* II, 890–900 [10] *ibid.* IV, 800–809 [11] Jonathan Richardson *Early Lives* (1734) [12] Milton 'Il Penseroso' [13] Milton *Arcades* [14] *Paradise Lost* V, 618–27 [15] John Dryden 'A Song for St Cecilia's Day' [16] *Paradise Lost* IX, 351–2 [17] Basil Willey *The Seventeenth Century Background* (Chatto & Windus, 1934; also Penguin)

6

Preparing for the Great Work

In 1644, John Milton published a short pamphlet called *Of Education*. In the middle of the Civil War, it was a return to earlier concerns and a looking forward to what he believed to be the needs of a new society. He set out a plan for a private academy, which would remedy the weaknesses of the universities. In the pamphlet, he defined education:

> *The end then of learning is to repair the ruin of our first parents by regaining to know God aright, and out of that knowledge to love him, to imitate him, to be like him, as we may the nearest by possessing our souls of true virtue, which being united to the heavenly grace of faith makes up the highest perfection.*[1]

Adam and Eve, in the myth, ate the fruit of the Tree of Knowledge of Good and Evil. Their disobedience let evil into the world that God had made. Learning, then, was a way back, through understanding, to God. It was an approach, from our imperfect state, to the perfection that is the quality of God. Notice the way in which Milton links the endeavour of learning with faith.

When he was nineteen, Milton wrote a poem called 'At a Vacation Exercise'. It was just that. It was an experiment and yet even at this age he seems to have held mighty ambitions:

> *Yet I had rather if I were to chuse,*
> *Thy service in some greater subject use,*
> *Such as may make thee search they coffers round,*
> *Before thou cloath my fancy in fit sound:*
> *Such were the deep transported mind may soare*
> *Above the wheeling poles, and at Heav'ns dore*
> *Look in, and see each blissful Deitie.*[2]

Much later, looking back to the time when he achieved his legal majority, Milton wrote:

> *And long it was not after, when I was confirmed in this opinion, that he who would not be frustrate of his hope to write*

well hereafter in laudable things, ought himself to be a true poem; that is a composition of the best and honourablest things.[3]

THE RÔLE OF THE POET

How then did Milton see his rôle in life? In 1641, in what has become a famous passage, exalted by the great events in England that could herald the millenium and the rule of the saints, Milton wrote in a prayer:

> *Then amidst the Hymns, and Hallelujahs of Saints some one may perhaps be heard offering at high strains in new and lofty Measures to sing and celebrate thy divine Mercies, and marvellous Judgments in this Land throughout all ages.*[4]

Such then was the guiding ambition, though remember that his great epic poems were written after the Restoration and the destruction of his earlier millenial hopes.

He first thought that his great work was to have an English theme but what? He considered very seriously using the legendary story of King Arthur and his knights but the idea did not last. It had first appeared in 1638 but by 1641 Milton clearly had abandoned the notion. It made little sense as England moved towards civil war. Real events loomed larger than the shadows of romantic legend. Besides, the subject was too much like that of Spenser's *Faerie Queene*. That great poem, whatever else it was, was no epic. In any case, Milton felt he was able to celebrate the achievements of his country and countrymen in prose. He wrote in Latin his two *Defences of the English People*. At the end of the Second Defence, he sees himself as a maker of history:

> *I have delivered my testimony, I would almost say, have erected a monument, that will not readily be destroyed, to the reality of those singular and mighty achievements which were above all praise. As the epic poet, who adheres at all to the rules of that species of composition, does not profess to describe the whole life of the hero whom he celebrates, but only some particular action of his life, as the resentment of Achilles at Troy, the return of Ulysses, or the coming of Aeneas into Italy; so it will be sufficient, either for my justification or apology, that I have heroically celebrated at least one exploit of my countrymen.*[5]

He had to think again about the subject of his epic poem. We can perhaps see how he arrived at *Paradise Lost* if we look at his own view of the nature of poetry.

We have seen that he believed that a poet must be a good man. Why? There had been a great deal of argument in the Elizabethan period about the nature of poetry. This was a period in which Greek learning and philosophy was transforming men's minds. Plato had attacked poetry vigorously. It was a deceiver. The visible world and all in it were imperfect, a pale reflection, if you like, of perfection. Poetry was an imitation, an attempted copy, of the real world. It was not one but two removes from perfection. It is not difficult to see how the Platonic dislike of poetry linked with Puritan feelings that poetry was dangerously sensual and probably immoral.

One way of countering this was simply to assert that poetry could enshrine moral truths. Because poetry is pleasing so the moral truths would be more palatable. This is not really a very effective defence of the art. Sir Philip Sidney in his *Defence of Poesy*, in discussing Plato, thinks of him not as an imitator of something out there in the real world but as a creator. The poet sees through, as it were, the outward appearance of things to the inward reality or virtue. In that sense, the poet is closer to perfection or to God, not farther away:

> *Only the poet, disdaining to be tied to any such subjection, lifted up with the vigour of his own invention, doth grow, in effect, into another nature, in making things either better than nature bringeth forth, or, quite anew, forms such as were never in nature . . . Nature never set forth the earth in so rich tapestry as divers poets have done; neither with pleasant rivers, fruitful trees, sweet-smelling flowers, nor whatsoever else may make the too-much-loved earth more lovely; her world is brazen; the poets only deliver a gold.*[6]

'*The poets only deliver a gold.*' This is a key idea, perhaps strange to modern ears. It is the function of the poet to discern the ideal, perhaps to urge men to right action, certainly to reveal the patterns underlying life which wickedness and confusion have muddied.

Milton was broadly in agreement with this view of the poet's rôle:

> *These abilities, wheresoever they be found, are the inspired gift of God rarely bestowed, but yet to some (though most abuse) in every Nation: and are of power beside the office of a pulpit, to inbreed and cherish in a great people the seeds of virtue, and public civility, to allay their perturbations of the*

mind, and set the affections in right tune, to celebrate in glorious and lofty Hymns the throne and equipage of God's Almightiness, and what he works, and what he suffers to be wrought with high providence in his Church.[7]

This particular passage, which occurs a little surprisingly in a pamphlet attacking episcopacy (*The Reason of Church Government*) goes on to attack '*the writings and interludes of libidinous and ignorant poetasters*' and how they '*do for the most part lap up vicious principles in sweet pills to be swallowed down, and make the taste of virtuous documents harsh and sour*'.[7]

Note the language Milton uses in both the above quotations. As well as the fairly conventional view of the moral rôle of the poet, there is an awareness of a unique quality of poetry not to be found in prose. The poem is a hymn, it seeks sweetness and its effect on the emotions is essentially harmonious. The bad poet makes disharmony of virtue.

Now this is of the very nature of poetry. The poet does not appeal to intellectual reason but to the passions. He works through the senses and can only work by giving delight.

It is very important to remember this as you read Milton. Because of his subject matter, there is a temptation to think too much in terms of his logic, of his ideas, of his beliefs. There is a temptation to think of *Paradise Lost* as if it were a kind of tract in poetic numbers. Of course, Milton brought to *Paradise Lost* a complexity of beliefs about God and about Man and it is useful to understand the range and context of these ideas and even, at times, to notice inconsistencies in them. But these are poems written to delight the reader—'*to allay the perturbations of the mind and set the affections in right tune*'. It is in Milton's *prose* works that we find the development of his thought. In the poems, this thinking is part of a larger whole, part of the experience that Milton brought to bear.

So what we are considering as we continue to look at the way in which Milton prepared himself for his great work is the raw material. His profound knowledge of the classics, of human and divine history, and of the Bible was like the great stone from which a sculptor carves his statue.

THE CLASSICS

Until quite recently the classical writings of Greece and Rome were the stuff of education. To be educated was, in part, to be wholly familiar with this body of legend. References to gods and men of ancient times came readily and naturally. It is not easy to think of a modern parallel for we have not yet acquired or developed any comparable body of myths that can serve the same necessary purposes. The need is there and it is possible to see uncertain and temporary ways of meeting that need.

For the myths of Greece and Rome helped men to make sense of life. They were not seen in historical perspective. Their relationship to ancient mysteries and religions was not important. They were not an anthropological quarry. They were about good and evil, about the workings of fate, about courage in adversity, about the heroic virtues, about the love of men and women mirrored in the gods, about death and rebirth. They were a source of strength to men as they went about their daily business in the uncertainties of the seventeenth century. And the stories were to be found, not in scraps of ballads or in the oral tradition of villages, but in a great literature. They were in the Greek of Homer and the Latin of Virgil and Ovid.

Yet these stories were far from being the whole of education. Far more important for life was the Bible. Indeed, as the century moved on, there were men who began to feel that the classical myths had little meaning for a Christian. After all, they were fictions while

17. *Judgment of Paris* by Rubens, 1638. This painting is both classical and pastoral but is also contemporary. The great Flemish artist Peter Paul Rubens lived in England for many years when, among other things, he painted the ceiling of Inigo Jones's Palace of Whitehall. (Reproduced by courtesy of the Trustees, The National Gallery, London)

the Bible was true. As Cowley, a literary figure of Milton's time, put it, the myths were '*at best . . . the confused antiquated dreams of senseless Fables and Metamorphoses*'. They no longer had much value for the serious writer. It is '*almost impossible to serve up any new Dish of that kinde. They are all but the Cold-meats of the Antients, new-heated, and new set forth.*' They were no better, thought Cowley, than the romantic nonsense of knight-errantry. The only lasting source of moral examples was the Bible and it could furnish subject matter for epic poetry in modern times.

This was not quite Milton's view. He still found the old tales a store from which truth might be extracted. Here is an example from *Areopagitica*:

> *Good and evil we know in the field of this World grow up together inseparably; and the knowledge of good is so involved and interwoven with the knowledge of evil, and in so many cunning resemblances hardly to be discerned, that those confused seeds which were imposed on Psyche as an incessant labour to cull out, and sort asunder, were not more intermixed. It was from out the rind of one apple tasted, that the knowledge of good and evil as two twins cleaving together leaped forth into the World. And perhaps this is that doom which Adam fell into of knowing good and evil, that is to say of knowing good by evil.*[8]

As Dr Tillyard commented in *Milton* (Peregrine edition, 1968) the classical and the biblical legends are mentioned in exactly the same tone. Yet Milton certainly did not believe the story of Psyche to be other than a fiction.

We can perhaps get the placing right by looking at the opening lines of *Paradise Lost*. Older peoples seemed to feel instinctively that man was nearer to God on top of a mountain. In his opening prayer for inspiration Milton refers to four hills:

> *Sing Heav'nly Muse, that on the secret top*
> *Of* Oreb, *or of* Sinai, *didst inspire*
> *That Shepherd, who first taught the chosen Seed,*
> *In the Beginning how the Heav'ns and Earth*
> *Rose out of* Chaos*: Or if* Sion *Hill*
> *Delight thee more, and* Siloa's *Brook that flowd*
> *Fast by the Oracle of God; I thence*
> *Invoke thy aid to my adventrous Song,*
> *That with no middle flight intends to soar*

Above th' Aonian *Mount; while it persues*
Things unattempted yet in Prose or Rime.[9]

There are three biblical hills to one classical—the home of the Muses. Milton tends to rise above the Greek mountain. His inspiration must come from richer sources than the ancient Muses can supply.

THE BIBLE

> *Every believer has a right to interpret the scriptures for himself, inasmuch as he has the Spirit for his guide, and the mind of Christ is in him.*[10]

> . . . '*all scripture is given by inspiration of God, and is profitable for doctrine, for reproof, for correction, for instruction in righteousness*'[10] quoted by Milton from the 2nd Epistle to Timothy.

> *The Scriptures, therefor, partly by reason of their own simplicity, and partly through the divine illumination, are plain and perspicuous in all things necessary to salvation, and adapted to the instruction even of the most unlearned, through the medium of diligent and constant reading.*[10]

The final quotation from *Christian Doctrine* is a classical statement of the Puritan view of the Bible. The picture one has from Puritan writings (such as those of Bunyan, for example) is of the man on his own, straining his eyes at the Bible by candlelight long after the profane have gone to bed, striving to understand the ways of God from His word and to stay, through that knowledge, on the narrow path to salvation.

Milton, however, was always insistent on the believer's right to interpret the Scriptures for himself. This was in line with much Protestant thinking; priestly intermediaries were to be rejected; a man must stand alone before his Maker. Yet the Miltonic emphasis is a strong one; it seems to be asserting an independence of judgment that goes beyond the kind of prayerful and sometimes anguished or incomprehending acceptance of the Word to be found in some other Puritans.

In fact, Milton, within limits, brought to the Bible a strong rational and critical sense. Though he accepted the doctrine of

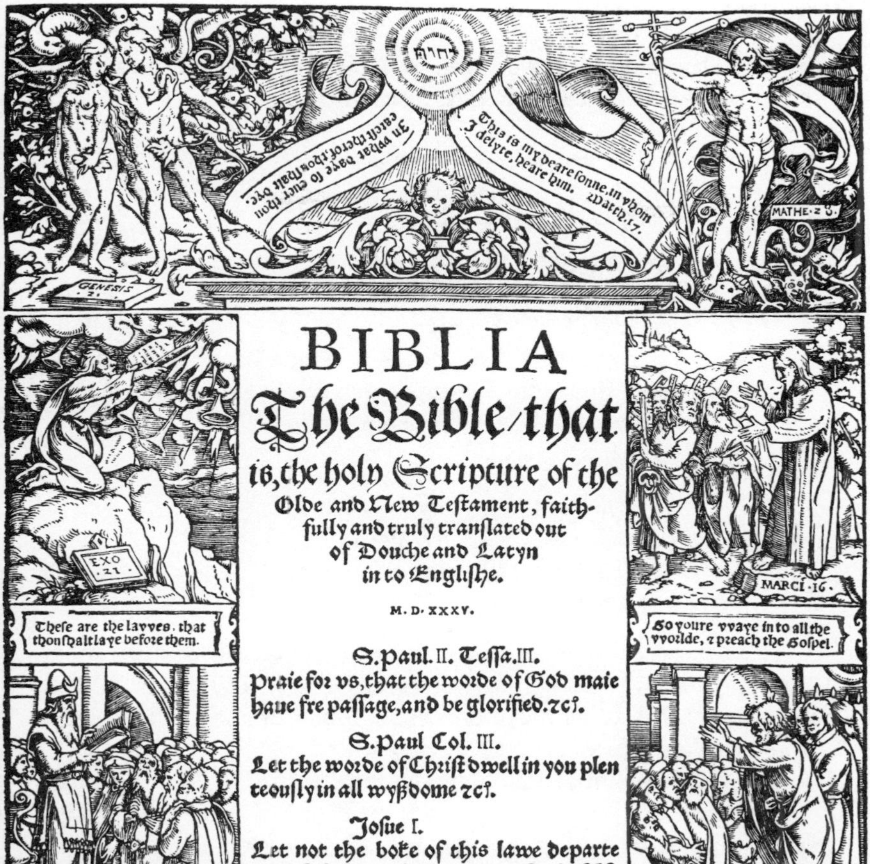

18. The title page of Coverdale's Bible, 1535. This translation was one of the first to be printed in English and was treasured by Protestants. Notice the woodcuts that summarize the salvation to be found within (Fotomas Index).

scriptural infallibility (every line was *true*) he saw that truth was often presented figuratively. He speaks thus of God:

> *Our safest way is to form in our minds such a conception of God as shall correspond with His own delineation and representation of Himself in the sacred writings. For granting that both in the literal and figurative descriptions of God, he is exhibited* not as He really is, *but in such a manner as may be within the scope of our comprehension, yet we ought to entertain such a conception of him, as He*, in condescending to accommodate Himself to our capacities, *has shown that he desires we should conceive . . .*[10] (my emphasis)

As Raphael says to Adam:

> *what surmounts the reach*
> *Of human sense, I shall delineat so,*
> *By lik'ning spiritual to corporeal forms,*
> *As may express them best.*[11]

In any case, the Bible had come to seventeenth-century man through many hands—translators and editors. This is an added uncertainty. It leaves little option but to follow our own consciences in interpretation.

The freedom is remarkable by the standards of the age in which Milton grew up. But it is very much in accord with the developing spirit of the latter half of the century—the age of the Royal Society and of rational theology. The Bible was becoming not the sole fountain of all literal truth, but a source wherein a man might discover something of the nature of God and lessons for the proper conduct of life. Milton was pointing down that road.

Yet, Milton did feel that contact with the Bible was, in a special way, contact with Truth. After all, he spent laborious years in Biblical analysis, text by text. Where else could a poet of Milton's cast of mind and heart go for inspiration? Where else could he find the subject matter, the life-giving stories and examples? As Basil Willey commented:

> *The existence of the Hebrew scriptures, then, in the particular setting of seventeenth century protestantism, must be accounted, together with the idea of the heroic poem, as the cause which made possible a great serious poem at just the period when poetry was coming to be thought of as elegant and agreeable rather than 'true'.*[12]

THE CHOICE OF SUBJECT

We have already seen that Milton's first notion of an epic was Arthurian. We have suggested some of the reasons why this idea seemed, after a while, inadequate. There is some evidence that he was also thinking of writing a tragedy. He had already, in *Comus*, written dramatically. He was aware of both Shakespeare and Ben Jonson. But then, the closing of the theatres by Parliament in 1642 would have postponed such an ambition, even if it were for a drama on a biblical theme, such as the Fall. Clearly, ideas continued to run through his head in the forties and fifties of the century and, equally clearly, the work he undertook for the Cause prevented any sustained effort at writing either epic or tragedy. Indeed, as millenial enthusiasm showed, if Milton had written his epic in the forties, it would have been no tragedy but a celebration of Divine Providence and the working out in England of God's plan for his creation, Man. We have to see *Paradise Lost* in the context of the bitter disappointment of political hopes. And this was a disappointment that was only confirmed by the return of Charles II; the Cromwellian era had brought its own disillusionments.

It is also true that Milton's whole character inclined him to a biblical subject. The subject had to be the Fall as this was the moment in human history from which all else sprang. Nor did it need the young Quaker, Ellworthy, to suggest to Milton his next poem. The counter-force to the disobedience of Adam and its consequences, was Christ. So *Paradise Lost* and *Paradise Regained* are part of a divine plan which is not yet complete.

THE FALL

John Donne, in his later years, wrote on his sick bed:

We thinke that Paradise and Calvarie,
Christs Crosse and Adams tree, stood in one place;
Looke Lord, and finde both Adams met in me;
As the first Adams sweat surrounds my face,
May the last Adams blood my soule embrace.[13]

There was no contemporary argument about the facts of the Fall. The story is in the Bible, both in Genesis and in scattered references in other books. Milton without doubt accepted the story as fact. But the Fall is more than a story or even an allegory; it is a doctrine. It is the statement that Man is a sinner, indeed born a sinner. Sin,

1.Cor.11,8.

*Or, Mannes, because she cometh of man: for in Ebr Ish, is man, and Ishah the woman.

Mat.19,5. mar.10,7. 1.cor.6,16. ephes.5,31.

p So that mariage requireth a greater duetie of vs towarde ẏ wiues, thē otherwise we are bounde to shewe to our parents.

23 Then the man said, *This now is bone
of my bones, and flesh of my flesh. She
shalbe called *woman, because she was ta-
ken out of man.
24 *Therefore shal man leaue p his father
and his mother, and shal cleaue to his wife,
and they shalbe one flesh.
25 And they were bothe naked, the man &
his wife, and were not q ashamed.

q For before sinne entred, all things were honest and comely.

THE SITVACION OF THE GARDEN OF EDEN.

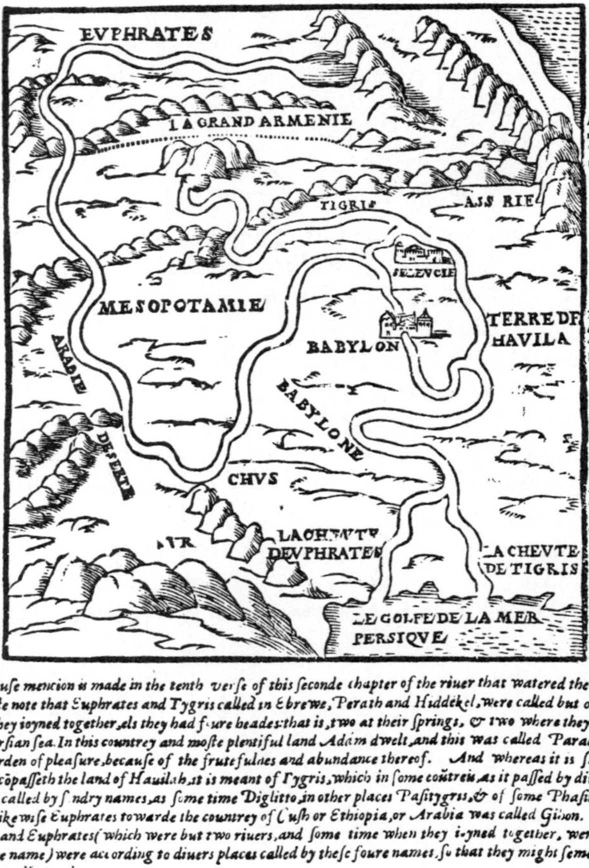

La grand Armenie. *Or, Armenia the great.

Terre de Hauiláh. *Or, land of Hauiláh.

La cheute d Euphrates *Or, the fall of Euphrates.

La cheute de Tygris. *Or, the fall of Tygris

Le golfe de la mer Persique *Or, the golfe of the Persian sea.

Because mencion is made in the tenth verse of this seconde chapter of the riuer that watered the garden, we muste note that Euphrates and Tygris called in Ebrewe, Perath and Hiddékel, were called but one riuer where they ioyned together, els they had foure heades: that is, two at their springs, & two where they fel into the Persian sea. In this countrey and moste plentiful land Adám dwelt, and this was called Paradise: that is, a garden of pleasure, because of the frutefulnes and abundance thereof. And whereas it is said that Pishón cōpasseth the land of Hauiláh, it is meant of Tygris, which in some cōutreis, as it passed by diuers places, was called by sundry names, as some time Diglitto, in other places Pasitygris, & of some Phasin or Pishón. Likewise Euphrates towarde the countrey of Cush or Ethiopia, or Arabia was called Gihón. So that Tygris and Euphrates (which were but two riuers, and some time when they ioyned together, were called after one name) were according to diuers places called by these foure names, so that they might seme to haue bene foure diuers riuers.

CHAP. III.

The womā seduced by the serpēt. 6 Entiseth her housbād to sinne. 14 They thre are punished. 15 Christ is promised. 19 Man is dust. 22 Man is cast out of paradise.

Wisdo. 2,25.

a As Satan cā change him selfe into an Angel of light, so did he abuse the wisdome of the serpent to deceaue man.

b God suffered Satan to make the serpent his instrument and to speake in him.

c In douting of Gods threatnig, she yelded to Satan.

1 NOw *the serpent was more a subtil
then anie beast of the field, which ẏ
Lord God had made: and he b said to the
woman, Yea, hathe God in dede said, Ye
shal not eat of euerie tre of the garden?
2 And the woman said vnto the serpēt, We
eat of the frute of the trees of the garden,
3 But of the frute of the tre, which is in the
middes of the garden, God hathe said, Ye
shal not eat of it, nether shal ye touche it,
c lest ye dye.
4 Then *the serpent said to the woman, Ye
shal not d dye at all,
5 But God doeth knowe, that when ye shal
eat thereof, your eyes shalbe opened, & ye
shalbe as gods, e knowing good and euil.
6 So the woman (seing that the tre was
good for meat, and that it was pleasant to
the eyes, & a tre to be desired to get know-
ledge) toke of the frute thereof, and did
*eat, and gaue also to her housband with
her, and he f did eat.
7 Then the eyes of them bothe were ope-
ned, & they g knewe that they were naked,
and they sewed figtre leaues together, and
made them selues *breeches.
8 ¶ Afterwarde they heard the voyce of

2.Cor.11,3.

d This is Satans chiefest subtiltie, to cause vs not to feare Gods threatenings.

e As thogh he shulde say, God doeth not forbid you to eat of the frute, saue that he knoweth that if you shulde eat thereof, you shulde be like to him.

Ecclus.25,33. 1.tim.2,14.

f Not so muche to please his wife, as moued by ambicion at her persuasion.

g They began to fele their miserie, but they soght not to God for remedie

*Ebr. things to girde about them to hide their priuities.

a.ii.

19. Page from the Geneva Bible, 1560, showing the verse that gave it the nickname the 'Breeches Bible'. Elizabeth Minshull owned a copy of this translation (The Mansell Collection)

since the Fall, is an inescapable condition of all human life. It is only through Christ that the consequences of sin can be escaped by any human being. So far, the doctrine is straightforward and hard. But there are still many questions—questions that the Bible story simply did not answer.

What is human nature? What is sin? What, indeed, was Adam's sin? Milton had to answer those questions if the writing of *Paradise Lost* was to be possible.

First of all, here is the Bible story in the language of the King James Bible:

> *And the Lord God planted a garden eastward in Eden; and there he put the man he had formed. And out of the ground made the Lord God to grow every tree that is pleasant to the sight, and good for food; the tree of life also in the midst of the garden, and the tree of knowledge of good and evil. . . .*
>
> *And the Lord God took the man, and put him into the garden of Eden to dress it and to keep it. And the Lord God commanded the man, saying: Of every tree of the garden thou mayest freely eat: But of the tree of the knowledge of good and evil, thou shalt not eat it: for in the day that thou eatest thereof thou shalt surely die. . . .*
>
> *Now the serpent was more subtil than any beast of the field which the Lord God had made. And he said unto the woman, Yea, hath God said, Ye shall not eat of every tree of the garden? And the woman said unto the serpent, We may eat of the fruit of the trees of the garden: But of the fruit of the tree which is in the midst of the garden, God hath said, Ye shall not eat of it, neither shall ye touch it, lest ye die.*
>
> *And the serpent said to the woman, Ye shall not surely die: For God doth know that in the day ye eat thereof, then your eyes shall be opened, and ye shall be as gods, knowing good and evil.*
>
> *And when the woman saw that the tree was good for food and that it was pleasant to the eyes, and a tree to be desired to make one wise, she took of the fruit thereof, and did eat, and gave also to her husband with her, and he did eat.*
>
> *And the eyes of them both were opened, and they knew that they were naked.*[14]

The punishment followed, expulsion from Eden, a life of work followed by death.

Now what was Milton to make of this story? What he did make of it hardly fits the Bible story, nor could it. For Adam and Eve fell, firstly through simple disobedience and, secondly through something that the Church had for long called the sin of Pride. The serpent suggested that *knowledge* would make man wise, make man himself a *god.*

This runs straight against Milton's own beliefs. To him, knowledge, reason, free choice are *good.* In the fable, they are the source of all our woe. Michael explains to Adam after the Fall what are its consequences for Man:

> *yet know withall,*
> *Since thy original lapse, true Libertie*
> *Is lost, which alwayes with right Reason dwells*
> *Twinnd, and from her hath no dividual being:*
> *Reason in man obscur'd, or not obeyd,*
> *Immediately inordinate desires*
> *And upstart Passions catch the Government*
> *From Reason, and to servitude reduce*
> *Man till then free.*[15]

This is part of a passage quoted in Chapter 3 for Michael goes on to link this loss of personal freedom to the loss of political liberty and to tyranny. Here is the same point from *Christian Doctrine*:

> *The loss, or at least the obscuration to a great extent of that right reason which enabled man to discern the chief good, and in which consisted as it were the life of the understanding . . . It consists, secondly, in that deprivation of righteousness and liberty to do good, and in that slavish submission to sin and the devil, which constitutes, as it were, the death of the will.*[16]

[1] Milton *Of Education* (1644) [2] Milton 'At a Vacation Exercise' [3] Milton *Apology for Smectymnuus* (1642) [4] Milton *Of Reformation Touching Church Discipline in England* (1641) [5] Milton *Defensio Secunda pro Populo Anglicano* (1654) [6] Sir Philip Sydney *Defence of Poesy* (*circa* 1583) [7] Milton *The Reason of Church Government* (1641) [8] Milton *Areopagitica* (1644) [9] *Paradise Lost* I, 6–16 [10] Milton *De Doctrina Christiana* (*circa* 1655–60) [11] *Paradise Lost* V, 571–4 [12] Basil Willey *The Seventeenth Century Background* (Chatto & Windus, 1934; also Penguin) [13] John Donne 'Hymn to God my God in my Sicknesse' [14] Genesis 2 vv. 8–9, 15–17; 3 vv. 1–7 [15] *Paradise Lost* XII, 82–90 [16] Milton *De Doctrina Christiana* (*circa* 1655–60)

7

Paradise Lost and Regained

What supports me, dost thou ask?
The conscience, Friend, to have lost them overply'd
In Liberties defence, my noble task,
Of which all Europe talks from side to side.
This thought might lead me through the worlds vain mask
Content though blind, had I no better guide.[1]

It was in 1652 that Milton became totally blind, the year in which his third daughter Deborah was born and his first wife, Mary Powell, died. The quotation above is from Sonnet XXII which was written three years later and shows a John Milton restored to his old determination, his old sense of a pre-ordained purpose to his life.

The great poems (*Paradise Lost*, *Paradise Regained* and *Samson Agonistes*) were written by a blind man. The visual imagery, then, of all three poems comes from Milton's memory of when he was not blind or from books recollected or read to him. The poetry itself was *dictated* by Milton to an amanuensis. He could compose some forty to fifty lines at a time in his head and hold them in his memory until they could be dictated. He made corrections when the lines were read back to him. More perhaps than any previous poetry or most that followed, Milton's was produced to be *heard*. The test of this poetry must be in reading aloud rather than in observation of its printed form. This is not to suggest any indifference on Milton's part to the printed form. As we shall see in Chapter 9, he was extremely fussy about the quality of his text, especially spelling and punctuation. He wanted the printed text to show, through its spelling and punctuation, as far as they could, how he wanted his lines *spoken*.

THE BEGINNING

We saw in the last chapter some of the reasons which led Milton to his choice of subject matter for his epic. We look now at some of the consequences of that choice. In particular, we look at the way Milton handles the basic myth and the kind of universe he constructs.

There is one further preliminary point. The beginning of an epic, by classical precedent, is a prayer to the Muses for inspiration. Characteristically, Milton follows the precedent yet transmutes it to something quite different. His invocation, at the opening of Book I is indeed a prayer. In a sense it makes the whole enterprise a prayer, an offering to God. The prayer, or invocation, is renewed at each major stage in the whole poem—at the beginning of Book III when we turn our eyes back from Hell to God and His purposes, at the beginning of Book VII where Raphael tells Adam of the Creation. The first movement of the poem is Hell—the Fall of Lucifer and his plan to subvert the new creation. The second movement speaks of the purposes of God. The third movement tells of life in Paradise. The final movement starts in Book IX. Milton pauses to look back at his own preparation for his task, to gather his forces again to recount the drama of man's disobedience and the consequences.

Paradise Regained then becomes a continuation of the same poem:

> *I who ere while the happy Garden sung,*
> *By one mans disobedience lost, now sing*
> *Recoverd Paradise to all mankind,*
> *By one mans firm obedience fully tri'd*
> *Through all temptation, and the Tempter foild*
> *In all his wiles, defeated and repulst,*
> *And* Eden *rais'd in the vast Wilderness.*[2]

Compare the opening of *Paradise Lost*:

> *Of Mans First Disobedience, and the Fruit*
> *Of that Forbidd'n Tree, whose mortal tast*
> *Brought Death into the World, and all our woe,*
> *With loss of* Eden, *till one greater Man*
> *Restore us, and regain, the blissful Seat,*
> *Sing Heav'nly Muse.*[3]

The correspondences are deliberately exact. So are they in the endings to the two poems. At the end of *Paradise Lost* we see Adam and Eve, expelled from Eden, moving into the world of work, struggle and death:

> *The World was all before them, where to choose*
> *Thir place of rest, and Providence thir guide:*

They hand in hand with wandring steps and slow,
Through Eden *took this solitarie way.*[4]

Christ defeats, in the Wilderness, all the wiles of the Tempter. Heaven rejoices and we are again left with an image of man.

Hail Son of the most High, heir of both Worlds,
Queller of Satan, on thy glorious work
Now enter, and begin to save mankind.
Thus they the Son of God our Saviour meek
Sung Victor, and from Heav'nly Feast refresht
Brought on his way with joy; hee unobserv'd
Home to his Mothers house privat returnd.[5]

20. Illustration for Book I of Satan cast down from Heaven, from the 1688 edition of *Paradise Lost* by Medina (Cambridge University Library)

The epic, then, is very carefully organized or planned. It moves from opening to conclusion with great assurance. It is to this organization and the problems Milton had in matching his raw material to his plan that we now turn.

THE MYTH, THE READER AND MILTON

Paradise Lost, then, moves from the Fall from Heaven to the Fall from Paradise and thence to the effect of the Fall upon mankind. It is, however, not just a *narrative*. Milton constantly, through the poem, reminds us of our present; he constantly relates events in the myth to other myths, to events in history, to the present state of man.

There is, further, a continuing *contrast* between the state before and after the Fall, the eating of the apple:

whose mortal tast
Brought Death into the World, and all our woe.

It is not that Adam and Eve were blissfully and innocently happy before and knew only suffering after. Man can know *both* joy and woe—or rather, he can see what joy might be. After all, Paradise was *lost*. It did not cease to exist. What was *regained* through Christ was the possibility of finding again that joy that is the natural condition of God's creation.

The presentation of this theme involved Milton in difficulties with the myth of Genesis and a considerable extension of that rather short Biblical story. Milton, also, as we have seen, was no orthodox Christian. He did not, for example, believe in an immediate life after death. His Christ was not the equal of God '*of one substance with the Father, begotten before the worlds . . . Perfect God and Perfect Man*'. (Athanasian Creed). Again, in *Paradise Lost*, we find that God creates the world out of the primitive matter of chaos; after all there is a pretty solid and substantial heaven and hell. Certainly, this is not the creation of the first chapter of Genesis.

The whole enterprise of the poem compelled Milton to precision. He had to provide the definite when the Bible has only vague generalities. Sin and Death become creatures—guardians of hell-gate. Indeed, Sin is born full-grown from the head of Lucifer, an ingenious use by Milton of the Greek myth of Athene, Goddess of Wisdom, being born fully-armed from the head of Zeus. After the Fall, Sin and Death build an actual physical causeway from the gates of Hell to the World, for the passage of devils.

The events of the poem had to be presented concretely. It suited Milton's imagination to give the spiritual world material form. For a reader to accept the apparatus of the epic, Milton had to be reasonably consistent. We look now at five key problems: the Tree of Knowledge, the portrayal of God, the fall of the angels, the geography of heaven, hell and earth, and Milton's use of allegory.

THE TREE OF KNOWLEDGE

It is quite clear what sort of tree this is in the myth. It is a *magical* tree. Eating the apple magically and instantly converted ignorant innocence into '*knowledge of good and evil*'. If Milton were to follow the myth, consider the implications. At one level, he would have been saddled with Adam and Eve, not only innocent, but knowing nothing. What did Adam and Eve *do* in Eden before the Fall? Food was abundantly provided; there was no need for work, even if they knew how. What would they talk about? How could a poet represent their talk without referring to any of the normal conditions of human life? They were a couple without history, with no sense of any future and no conflict.

There was a worse problem. Milton could not possibly accept the myth at all. For the myth portrays the passive innocence before the Fall as the ideal state. Struggle and work are the evils brought to man by the Fall. As we have seen, Milton not only felt the necessity of effort, he also believed strongly in the moral power of independent thought. To him, the Fall was not the acquisition of knowledge. In particular it could not be the moral knowledge of the myth. The power to *reason* was a gift of God. For Milton, sin entailed the overthrow of reason by passion.

Milton handles this problem by putting the traditional view into the mouth of Satan! When Satan hears about the Tree of Knowledge, he is clearly surprised:

> *One fatal Tree there stands of Knowledge calld,*
> *Forbidd'n them to taste: Knowledge forbidd'n?*
> *Suspicious, reasonless. Why should thir Lord*
> *Envie them that? can it be sin to know,*
> *Can it be death? and do they onely stand*
> *By Ignorance, is that thir happie state,*
> *The proof of thir obedience and thir faith?*[6]

It was through insisting on the *magical* quality of the fruit that Satan tempted Eve. The serpent could speak because he had eaten of the fruit. If Adam and Eve ate the apple then they too would magically be able to understand all things. The very fact that they would understand both good and evil would mean they would the better be able to shun evil! Satan asks Eve to wonder why God had forbidden them to eat of the fruit:

Why then was this forbid? Why but to awe,
Why but to keep ye low and ignorant,
His worshippers; he knows that in the day
Ye Eate thereof, your Eyes that seem so cleere,
Yet are but dim, shall perfetly be then
Op'nd and cleerd, and yee shall be as Gods,
Knowing both Good and Evil as they know.[7]

21. Illustration for Book IX of the events of the Temptation shown in sequence in the one drawing, from the 1688 edition of *Paradise Lost* by Medina (Cambridge University Library)

22. *Eve Tempted by the Serpent* by William Blake, 1796 (Crown Copyright, Victoria and Albert Museum)

Adam and Eve were not, of course, in the poem, even before the Fall, the ignorant creatures of the myth. They were already living a remarkably human life, living as husband and wife, working (yes, working) in the garden and imbibing knowledge of their world and its creation from a special angelic teacher, the Archangel Raphael. It was from Raphael that they heard the stirring story of the fall of Lucifer himself.

However, Satan does choose the right temptation. Eve took the apple and Adam followed out of love for Eve, determined to share with her whatever would befall.

What then was their sin? What was, in Milton's view, the nature of the Fall?

By eating the fruit, Adam and Eve gained no new knowledge at all. Remember the very opening line of the poem?

Of Mans First Disobedience, and the Fruit
Of that Forbidd'n Tree . . .

The sin was disobedience and nothing else. In Milton's book on Christian doctrine, he discusses the story. He talks of an Adam and Eve knowing fully the laws of nature and having free will. There was nothing wrong in knowledge or in finding out. The Tree was forbidden because it was forbidden. Milton goes on to say:

> *It was necessary that something should be forbidden or commanded as a test of fidelity, and that an act of its own nature indifferent, in order that man's obedience might be thereby manifested.*[8]

As Basil Willey comments on this observation:

> *It was in this direction alone that the unfallen Adam could practise free choice, and the choice lay simply between obedience and disobedience.*[9]

If Satan was the *deceiver*, then the apple could give no magical access of knowledge. It too deceived. It was 'fallacious'. The result of eating was intoxication and sexual indulgence. Awaking and self-conscious, they hid:

> *Thus fenc't, and as they thought, thir shame in part*
> *Coverd, but not at rest or ease of Mind,*
> *They sate them down to weep, nor onely Teares*
> *Raind at thir Eyes, but high Winds worse within*
> *Began to rise, high Passions, Anger, Hate,*
> *Mistrust, Suspicion, Discord, and shook sore*
> *Thir inward State of Mind, calme Region once*
> *And full of Peace, now tost and turbulent:*
> *For Understanding rul'd not, and the Will*
> *Heard not her lore, both in subjection now*
> *To sensual Appetite, who from beneath*
> *Usurping over sovran Reason claimd*
> *Superior sway.*[10]

There can be no doubt what Milton saw as the Fall. It was a victory of the passions over reason, of subconscious forces over conscious control. It was, in this sense, profoundly a loss of *freedom*.

THE PORTRAYAL OF GOD

What manner of God does Milton draw for us? What God is it that could impose so capricious an interdict as that upon the Tree of Knowledge? The task was, in fact, an impossible one. If God is not only omnipotent but also omniscient, eternal and both just and benevolent, how could he be a character in a human epic? Homer had no such problem; his gods were human beings writ large. Milton's own God was more like a set of principles!

Theologians have always had to face the contradiction. They tried and still try to avoid thinking of God as if he were a kind of glorified human monarch. Yet how could he be described in a way meaningful to ordinary men without using the language of human experience? In *Paradise Lost* God has to be a character. He rules in a particular place—heaven—and he wages war against his enemies with real armies. The *machinery* was necessary but it could not possibly encompass profounder conceptions of God.

You will remember from the previous section that Milton interpreted the Fall as a victory of passion over reason. Adam had the freedom to choose to eat the apple. He chose enslavement to his passions rather than the freedom of serving God—that is, Reason. This makes sense if we think of God in terms of the law of reason. But it is a good deal less easy to accept if we think of God as a heavenly monarch issuing orders and prohibitions.

The story and Milton's best insights did not match at this key point and so there are always some difficulties when we read the speeches in heaven of God and Christ.

THE FALL OF THE ANGELS

It was much easier to deal with Lucifer and his hosts. There is not much in the Bible—just a few verses in Isaiah, readily misinterpreted:

> *How art thou fallen from heaven, O Lucifer, son of the morning! How art thou cut down to the ground, which didst weaken the nations!*
>
> *For thou hast said in thine heart, I will ascend into heaven, I will exalt my throne above the stars of God: I will sit also upon the mount of the congregation, in the sides of the north: I will ascend above the heights of the clouds; I will be like the most High.*
>
> *Yet thou shalt be brought down to hell, to the sides of the pit.*[11]

There are some references in Revelation and a mass of medieval legend building on these slight foundations. So Milton was able to make use of all these tales without the kind of danger he faced by including God among the dramatis personae. He was also helped by an early identification in the history of Christianity of the devils with pagan gods (found notably in St Jerome). This was a very handy notion. It gave the fallen angels *names* and showed them through history diverting man from the worship of the true God. In fact, the notion was both familiar and quite commonly accepted. Here is an Elizabethan theologian Hooker on this point:

> *The fall of the angels, therefore, was pride. Since their fall, their practices have been the clean contrary to those just mentioned. For, being dispersed, some in the air, some in the earth, some in the water, some among the minerals, dens and caves that are under the earth; they have by all means laboured to effect a universal rebellion against the laws, and as far as in them lieth utter destruction of the ways of God. These wicked spirits the heathen honoured instead of Gods, both generally under the name of* dii inferi *'gods infernal', and particularly, some in oracles, some in idols, some as household gods, some as nymphs; in a word, no foul or wicked spirit which was not one way or other honoured of men as god, till such time as light appeared in the world, and dissolved the works of the Devil.*[12]

Notice that the fall of these angels is ascribed to *pride*. They had turned from the worship of God to the worship of themselves. It is not surprising that Milton's Hell is so vivid a part of the poem. The mythology was ready to hand for him to mould in his imagination. A major section of Book I is a catalogue of the gods of old.

HEAVEN AND HELL

Milton was partly helped by existing notions. What we have in *Paradise Lost* is a modification of a traditional scheme. You will remember in Chapter 5, the description of Ptolemaic astronomy—the earth at the centre of the crystal spheres which governed the motions of the planets. Milton uses this concept. There are ten spheres. Nine of these are transparent—the spheres of the seven planets (including sun and moon), the sphere of the fixed stars and the crystalline sphere. The tenth sphere or *primum mobile* is opaque. The whole hangs by a golden chain from that exact point on the battlements of heaven where Lucifer fell. There is a rich staircase from Heaven to the tenth sphere that can be let down or taken up. There is an entrance through the tenth sphere giving access to the created universe and to the world at its centre.

This is but a small part of the cosmology. Heaven from which the spherical universe hangs is seen in *Paradise Lost* as a huge plain with its own geography of hills, valleys and rivers. God himself is located on a sacred cloud-hidden Mount. There are golden lamps—for heaven has both day and night. If this seems odd, remember the blindness of the poet deprived of the pleasures of dawn and dusk. Round the whole plain of heaven are sapphire battlements.

It was to the north of this plain that the rebellious Satan built his city. It survived three days before defeat and overthrow. Imagine now the *fall*. It took nine days through Chaos. This is the region, turbulent and dark, filled with the raw material of the universe. This raw material is not the traditional four elements of earth, air, fire and water but the even more basic parts of which the elements are composed—hot, cold, moist and dry. Until composed, these rudimentary particles are in turbulent conflict with each other.

Beneath Chaos is another great plain—this time the plain of Hell so vividly described in Book I. Thus, for Satan to reach Eden to tempt Adam and Eve, he must leave Hell and the shores of the infernal lake, pass through the gates of Hell, journey back across Chaos and arrive at the primum mobile below the battlements of Heaven. He must then enter through the one passageway and fly down through the spheres until he lands on earth itself.

A note now upon the inhabitants of Heaven and Hell. Milton again uses the traditional view as a basis. Medieval man saw the angels in a *hierarchy*. Each order of angels had its place in the hierarchy, the chain of being. As there were nine spheres below the primum mobile, so there were nine orders of angels below God. They were in three groups of three reflecting the divine Trinity. The highest order is that of Seraphs, Cherubs and Thrones, solely occupied in the ceaseless praise of God. Then come Dominations, Virtues and Powers. The third group is that of Principalities, Archangels and Angels and these are the spiritual bodies that carry out the *active* commands of the Deity. Milton is rather less precise than this. He keeps the notion of the hierarchies of heaven but promotes the archangels. These active beings are the commanders of the heavenly armies and supreme below God. There is a nice logic here in the mythology for Satan was an Archangel. And the fallen angels, devils, pagan deities, reflect in Hell the heavenly hierarchy which once was theirs.

The apparatus is not the poem. The poem is the conflict of mighty forces centring upon the soul of man. It is not a useful question to ask whether Milton believed his account of heaven, hell, and earth was true. What this material geography did was to clothe, make manifest to our *imaginations* the concepts of good and evil.

ALLEGORY

We have already briefly noted the porters of Hellgate—Sin and Death. Sin was born, like Athene, full grown from the head of Lucifer. Now these are *allegorical* figures and though Milton owes a small debt to Greek myth and a rather larger one to Spenser, they are the products of Milton's imagination—an original contribution to the poem's personae. There was, by Milton's time, an ancient tradition of allegory in literature. Early sixteenth century drama was peopled by personified vices and virtues. Langland's dream of Piers the Plowman set such vices and virtues against a very

23. Illustration for Book II from the 1688 edition of *Paradise Lost* by Medina (Cambridge University Library)

English background. It was an accepted way of investing abstract concepts with flesh and body. Perhaps the best-known example of allegory is Bunyan's *Pilgrim's Progress.* The journey of Christian through an English landscape peopled with vices and virtues speaking in the idiom of ordinary folk has itself a long history. The comparison of life to a pilgrimage was the staple of sermons in country churches for centuries.

However, to be successful, allegory must be convincing on both levels. The allegorical creature must convince as a creature; the moral story at the deeper level must also be consistent. Milton's use of allegory is rather different to that commonly found in English writing. Sin is the daughter of Satan, we are told. The lascivious beauty which ensnared Lucifer in heaven can now be seen for what it is in the portress of Hellgate.

Before the Gates there sat
On either side a formidable shape;
The one seemd Woman to the waste, and fair,
But ended foul in many a scaly fould
Voluminous and vast, a Serpent armd
With mortal sting: about her middle round
A cry of Hell Hounds never ceasing barkd
With wide Cerberean *mouths full loud, and rung*
A hideous Peal: yet, when they list, would creep,
If aught disturbd thir noise, into her woomb,
And kennel there, yet there still barkd and howld
Within unseen.[13]

This description derives from Spenser's *Faerie Queene.* The Red Cross Knight, accompanied by his Lady, travels through a wood. He comes to a dark den; the lady warns him that it is the den of *Error*. Foolhardy, the knight enters the den and sees a monstrous creature half woman, half serpent:

And as she lay upon the durtie ground,
Her huge long taile her den all overspred,
Yet was in knots and many boughtes upwound,
Pointed with mortall sting. Of her there bred
A thousand yong ones, which she dayly fed,
Sucking upon her poisonous dugs, each one
Of sundry shapes, yet all ill favoured:
Soon as that uncouth light upon them shone;
Into her mouth they crept, and suddain all were gone.[14]

Compare these two remarkably similar visions. Which is the more vivid and immediate to the senses? There can be no doubt that Milton's Sin is more vaguely conceived, less sharply realized than Spenser's. There is always a balance to be kept in allegory. If the description is too vivid we pay too little attention to the meaning. If the poet is too much concerned with the meaning the imaginative impact is lost.

HOW DO WE READ THE EPICS?

The allegory of Sin and Death suggests an unusual feature of Miltonic epic. The imagery, as we have seen, is large and powerful but it does not have the obvious narrative drive of Spenser. Milton is not primarily a *storyteller*. Look, for example, at lines 392–521 in Book I, where the fallen angels are mustered as the heathen gods. It is an evocative catalogue of classical learning and the story has to wait while the infernal legions pass. Again, in Book IX, when Adam and Eve awake to know their shame, they hide. And Milton provides a natural history lesson on fig trees to make sure we know what kind they pick to make the legendary fig leaves to clothe their nakedness. Again, the narrative has to wait upon the digression.

The epics are full of such digressions. It is not surprising that many readers have valued them not for the story but for their encyclopedic quality.

One needs to look at the digressions carefully to understand what Milton is doing. He is constantly, it seems to me, keeping the *perspective* before our eyes. There is little concern for narrative suspense; the story is well enough known anyway. But we do need to have present before us, all the time, the meaning of the events. The Fall symbolizes *all* human history. Christ's resistance to the temptations of Satan are the means whereby Paradise is regained for us. So there is a compelling need for each step in the story to be related at once to the larger context. Here is an example. At the end of Book II, Satan arrives below the battlements of Heaven to see the new created world for the first time:

Or in the emptier waste, resembling Air,
Weighs his spred wings, at leasure to behold
Farr off th'Empyreal Heav'n, extended wide
In circuit, undetermind square or round,
With Opal Towrs and Battlements adornd
Of living Saphire, once his native Seat;

And fast by hanging in a gold'n Chain
This pendant World, in bigness as a Starr
Of smallest Magnitude close by the Moon.
Thither full fraught with mischievous revenge,
Accurst, and in a cursed hour he hies.[15]

The lines refer back to the angelic fall and forward to the fall of man.

Only a few lines earlier, Milton interrupts the saga of Satan's journey through chaos to make us look forward to what was to happen after the Fall:

So hee with difficulty and labour hard
Mov'd on, with difficulty and labour hee;
But hee once past, soon after when Man fell,
Strange alteration! Sin and Death amain
Following his track, such was the will of Heav'n,
Pav'd after him a broad and beat'n way
Over the dark Abyss, whose boiling Gulf
Tamely endur'd a Bridge of wondrous length
From Hell continu'd reaching th'utmost Orbe
Of this frail World.[16]

Notice the characteristic Miltonic sentence structure here. It is wholly unlike normal written English, even of his own period. It keeps us held fast as Satan struggles on to think of the causeway. The syntax itself helps the interruption of the narrative by its contorted form. Milton was perfectly capable of writing directly though always given to grand effects. Earlier poems do not have this very personal syntactical style for it was developed specially for the epic.

[1] Milton 'Sonnet XXII' [2] *Paradise Regained* I, 1–7 [3] *Paradise Lost* I, 1–6 [4] *ibid.* XII, 646–9 [5] *Paradise Regained* IV, 633–9 [6] *Paradise Lost* IV, 514–20 [7] *ibid.* IX, 703–9 [8] Milton *De Doctrina Christiana* (*circa* 1655–60) [9] Basil Willey *The Seventeenth Century Background* (Chatto & Windus, 1934; also Penguin) [10] *Paradise Lost* IX, 1120–31 [11] Isaiah 14 vv. 12–15 [12] Richard Hooker *Of the Laws of Ecclesiastical Politie* (1594) [13] *Paradise Lost* II, 648–58 [14] Spenser *Faerie Queene* Book I Canto I Stanza 15 [15] *Paradise Lost* II, 1045–55 [16] *ibid.* 1021–30

8

The Language of Miltonic Epic

In 1611, John Milton was three years old. This was the year of publication of the King James Bible—the Authorized Version. About this time, Shakespeare wrote *The Winter's Tale* and *The Tempest*. John Donne was writing poetry; Tourneur's *The Atheists Tragedy* and Ben Jonson's *Bartholomew Fair* both appeared in 1611. So did Sir Walter Raleigh's *History of the World*.

John Milton was a Londoner and he was educated at St Paul's School which he entered the year before Shakespeare died. His youth therefore covered the dying fall of the Elizabethans and the new writing and changed sensibility of a new century.

No writer can be immune from the cultural atmosphere of his day. Perhaps what the greatest writers do is to change the way people look at life; they are architects of their own setting, at least in part. But even genius must use what is to hand as raw material. This is especially true of the young writer who is dependent, too, upon the *forms* and *styles* of writing that are about him. The story of a great writer is nearly always a story of trying out known forms, modifying, discarding and transforming them into his own personal style, his unique vision. It is this kind of story that we tell in this chapter.

MILTON AND THE ELIZABETHANS

When he was about 17, Milton wrote a poem called 'On the Death of a Fair Infant', perhaps about his niece Anne Phillips. Here is a stanza:

Or wert thou of the golden-winged host,
Who having clad thyself in human weed,
To earth from thy prefixed seat did post,
And after short abode flie back with speed,
As if to shew what creatures Heav'n doth breed,
   Thereby to set the hearts of men on fire
To scorn the sordid world, and unto Heav'n aspire.[1]

24. *The Arcadian Shepherds* by Nicholas Poussin, a pastoral painting. Even in this ideal Greek countryside the shepherds must face the reality of death. The convention and the classics assist the artist in conveying a universal feeling. Poussin's seriousness has affinities with Milton's serious use of the convention in 'Lycidas' (Courtauld Institute of Art for the Trustees of the Chatsworth Settlement)

The poem has eleven stanzas of this form. It is a remarkably self-assured and competent performance. It is conventional stuff for the time—he is influenced partly by Spenser and rather more by Elizabethan translations of Ovid. His early poems are often Elizabethan in tone, rather old-fashioned his contemporaries may have thought:

Fly envious Time, till thou run out thy race,
Call on the lazy leaden-stepping hours,
Whose speed is but the heavy Plummets pace;[2]

We must now say something about the pastoral convention. It may be a little less remote from our sensibility than it was ten or twenty years ago. There is certainly a late twentieth-century yearning for a rather romantic countryside, for a simple, non-industrial life. There have been experiments, not for the first time in urban history, by groups of people in setting up communes, rural and self-sufficient. The pleasures of the country are a commonplace desire of urban living.

Pastoral poetry is also largely urban and certainly literary and sophisticated. The Greek and Latin authors from whom the mode was taken were sophisticated writers and found the alleged simplicities of rural life a way of separating out from the complexities of ordinary life, certain feelings and desires.

There are other advantages in writing about shepherds and their flocks. The imagery occurs in the Bible. Christ is likened to a shepherd and men to his flock, good and bad. Secondly, a writer could use the convention of writing about shepherds and their life to talk about quite different matters. It was a valuable mask for satire or the expression of unfashionable views. Thirdly, pastoral poetry could readily be a kind of 'escapism'—a presentation of the ideal in a world that was far from perfect.

However, by the time Milton was writing poetry, the pastoral convention had largely faded away. As we shall see, the concerns of most seventeenth-century poets were more direct. The great master of the convention had been Spenser (1552–99). Milton acknowledged Spenser as his master in the writing of English verse. And Spenser, it was said by a friend, was 'following the example of the best and most ancient poets', that is, the Virgil of the *Eclogues* and the *Georgics*. It is worth noting, in passing, that Shakespeare's *As You Like It* is an example of the vitality of the convention, even in the London theatre.

Here is Spenser in his Eclogue for June in the *Shepheards Calender*:

Lo Colin, here the place, whose pleasaunt syte
From other shades hath weaned my wandring mynde.
Tell me, what wants me here to work delyte?
The simple ayre, the gentle warbling wynde,
So calme, so coole, as nowhere else I fynde:

The grassye ground with daintye Daysies dight,
The Bramble bush, where Birds of every kynde
To the waters fall their tunes atemper right.[3]

Compare this with these lines from Milton's 'L'Allegro':

Streit mine eye hath caught new pleasures
While the Lantskip round it measures,
Russet Lawns and Fallows Gray,
Where the nibling flocks do stray,
Mountains on whose barren brest
The labouring clouds do often rest:
Meadows trim with Daisies pide,
Shallow Brooks and Rivers wide.[4]

Spenser used the form in order to attack what he thought were the abuses of the Roman Church:

Tho under colour of shepheards, somewhile
There crept in Wolves, ful of fraude and guile,
That often devoured their owne sheepe,
And often the shepheards, that did them keepe.[5]

Milton wrote in the pastoral convention with complete seriousness in 'Lycidas', ostensibly a lament for a friend, Edward King, who had been drowned in the Irish Sea, but as much a meditation upon the state of England. His concern is with the Church of England:

How well could I have spar'd for thee young swain,
Anow of such as for their bellies sake,
Creep and intrude and climb into the fold![6]

'Lycidas' was published in 1638, a year after the publication of Milton's masque *Comus*. It is a remarkable and highly accomplished poem. Within the pastoral convention, Milton is developing his own unmistakable voice:

Ay me! Whilst thee the shores and sounding Seas
Wash far away, where ere thy bones are hurld,
Whether beyond the stormy Hebrides,
Where thou perhaps under the whelming tide
Visit'st the bottom of the monstrous world;
Or whether thou to our moist vows deny'd,
Sleep'st by the fable of Bellerus old,
Where the great vision of the guarded Mount
Looks towards Namancos and Bayona's hold;

25. *Mercury and Battus* by Claude Lorrain (1600–82) (Courtauld Institute of Art for the Trustees of the Chatsworth Settlement)

Look homeward Angel now, and melt with ruth,
And, O ye Dolphins, waft the haples youth.[7]

The pastoral is suffering a sea change. There is greater depth of feeling. There is also the complex sentence structure which keeps us waiting so long for the main clause. There is the natural and unforced learning. The reference is to a Cornish legend of a giant, Bellerus. The guarded Mount, then, is St Michael's. Edward King's body may be carried either to the far north or south to Penzance. The castle on St Michael's Mount looks far across the sea to Spain (*Namancos and Bayona's hold*), the home of the Inquisition. The point is that Milton rarely wastes words. It is a mistake, perhaps, to dwell too much on the *sound* of such a passage, impressive though it is. The reference to the legend makes a point both about Edward King and about the need to guard England against a Catholic threat.

Yet Milton never abandoned wholly the pastoral convention. He continued to use what he had learnt from Ovid and from the Elizabethan practitioners of this art. Where else came the descriptions of Eden in *Paradise Lost*? The Archangel visits Adam and Eve:

and now is come
Into the blissful field, through Groves of Myrrhe,
And flouring Odours, Cassia, Nard and Balme;

A Wilderness of sweets; for Nature here
Wantond as in her prime, and plaid at will
Her Virgin Fancies, pouring forth more sweet,
Wilde above Rule or Art; enormous bliss.[8]

Men yearn for a lost Eden, a Golden Age of the past with '*calm of mind all passion spent*' (*Samson Agonistes*). Poets and artists portray Arcadia as an ideal for which we should strive or to which we should return.

In Chapter 4 we saw Poussin's *Landscape with a Snake* (Fig. 14). Another artistic contemporary of Milton was the Frenchman Claude Lorrain (1600–82) who lived in Rome for most of his life. Compare the idealized classical landscape of his *Mercury and Battus* (Fig. 25).

MILTON AND THE METAPHYSICALS

The poetic temper of an uncertain yet exciting age was set by John Donne—the rake who gave up worldly advancement for a love match and whose passionate intellect led him then, as Dean, into the pulpit of St Paul's. Two worlds met in John Donne—the old medieval and Catholic certainties (he was of a Catholic family) and the topsy-turvy world of reformation and discovery. In the very imagery of his poetry, we can see both worlds, sparking across to each other like the poles of a giant condenser:

And now good morrow to our waking soules,
Which watch not one another out of feare;
For love, all love of other sights controules,
And makes one little roome, an everywhere.
Let sea-discoverers to new worlds have gone,
Let Maps to other, worlds on worlds have showne,
Let us possess one world, each hath one, and is one.[9]

In later years, John Donne was to write of the divine love in the imagery of human love:

Take me to you, imprison me, for I
Except you enthrall me, never shall be free,
Nor ever chaste, except you ravish me.[10]

The image works if its own passion stops us from thinking too much about it. Much of the religious poetry of the time was dramatic, almost shocking, and certainly very conscious of the paradoxes of religion—especially the thought of God becoming Man in Christ. So the Catholic poet, Richard Crashaw (1612–49):

Wellcome, all WONDERS in one sight!
Eternity shutt in a span.
Sommer in Winter. Day in Night.
Heaven in earth, and GOD in MAN.
Great little one! whose all-embracing birth
Lifts earth to heaven, stoopes heav'n to earth.[11]

Milton wrote his 'Ode on the Morning of Christ's Nativity' in 1629 when he was 21. He was, naturally enough, influenced by contemporary styles:

It was the Winter wilde,
While the Heav'n-born-childe,
All meanly wrapt in the rude manger lies;
Nature in awe to him
Had doff't her gaudy trim,
With her great Master so to sympathise:
It was no season then for her
To wanton with the Sun her lusty Paramour.

The pagan gods sense that the Nativity is their defeat:

The lonely mountain o're
And the resounding shore,
A voice of weeping heard, and loud lament;
From haunted spring, and dale
Edg'd with poplar pale,
The parting Genius is with sighing sent,
With flowre-inwov'n tresses torn
The Nymphs in twilight shade of tangled thickets mourn.[12]

This is quite unlike metaphysical verse. It already has a quality that we can recognize as Milton's. There is the classical knowledge, the suggestion of the pastoral (but much heavier than Spenser in its rhythms). The link, perhaps, is with *painting*. Almost any religious painting of the time quite naturally uses classical motifs. There is a very easy and natural mingling of the pagan and the Christian. Compare 'Lycidas':

There entertain him all the Saints above,
In solemn troops, and sweet Societies
That sing, and singing in their glory move,

And wipe the tears for ever from his eyes.
Now Lycidas *the Shepherds weep no more;*
Henceforth thou art the Genius of the shore,
In thy large recompense, and shalt be good
To all that wander in that perilous flood.[13]

Edward King is *both* in Heaven and a pagan deity guarding seamen. The two worlds co-exist in 'Lycidas' as they do no longer in *Paradise Lost* where the gods have become devils.

MILTON AND SHAKESPEARE

There were other styles with which the young Milton experimented. On 29th September 1634, his masque *Comus* was performed at Ludlow Castle, before the Earl of Bridgewater, then Lord President of Wales. Masques were very popular entertainments in noble households. They were part spectacles, part dramas, part operas. What Milton presented was a kind of morality play, an allegory of a lady separated from her two brothers in a wood and tempted to give up her chastity by Comus (a kind of Dionysus figure) and his villainous crew, only to be rescued well in time by the returning brothers. The form gave plenty of opportunity for elaborate outside settings, costume, song, some drama and many poetic speeches.

Comus is a rather odd production—partly because Milton used the opportunity to try out varied styles, including the dramatic. There are sections which are not unlike 'L'Allegro' or even the rhymed speech of the fairies in Shakespeare's *A Midsummer Night's Dream*. It is the blank verse that offers us the most interest. Some of it is fairly ordinary stage rhetoric:

Unmuffle ye faint stars, and thou fair Moon
That wonst to love the travailers benizon,
Stoop thy pale visage through an amber cloud,
And disinherit Chaos, that raigns here
In double night of darknes and of shades.[14]

There are other passages that have almost the metaphorical richness of the mature Shakespeare. Comus praises to the Lady the fertility of nature:

Wherefore did Nature powre her bounties forth,
With such a full and unwithdrawing hand,
Covering the earth with odours, fruits and flocks,

Thronging the Seas with spawn innumerable,
But all to please and sate the curious taste?
And set to work millions of spinning worms,
That in their green shops weave the smooth-hair'd silk
To deck her Sons, and that no corner might
Be vacant of her plenty, in her own loyns
She hutch't th'all worshipt ore, and precious gems
To store her children with.[15]

The whole speech is well worth the reading. Milton obviously had read the great dramatists, Ben Jonson as well as Shakespeare. But what about this?

Bacchus that first from out the purple grape,
Crush't the sweet poison of misused Wine,
After the Tuscan Mariners transform'd
Coasting the Tyrrhene shore, as the winds listed,
On Circes Iland fell (who know not Circe
The daughter of the Sun? Whose charmed cup
Whoever tasted, lost his upright shape,
And downward fell into a grovelling Swine)[16]

The first full stop comes *twenty-four* lines later! In fact, this long passage is not especially difficult to grasp *read aloud*. But we can see the beginnings of the move to the complex and often inverted sentence structure of *Paradise Lost*.

It is worth noting here that Milton retained his interest in drama as a form. You will remember that an early plan for *Paradise Lost* itself was dramatic. This ambition was fulfilled at the end of his life in *Samson Agonistes*—though this is more Greek in form.

THE MATURE BLANK VERSE

The Measure is English Heroic Verse without Rime, as that of Homer in Greek, and of Virgil in Latin . . . it rather is to be esteemed as an example set, the first in English, of ancient liberty recoverd to Heroic Poem from the troublesom and modern bondage of Rimeing.[17]

The defence that prefaced *Paradise Lost* was necessary. Most writers and critics of the time assumed that rhyme was needed for any long and serious poem. But we have already noticed the strong Elizabethan influence on Milton—not just Spenser but the great

Elizabethan dramatists as well. Blank verse has a number of advantages for Milton's purposes. Here are some:

1 It is much easier to handle a long period with the sense running over the line endings.

2 There is greater freedom to place pauses and stresses as demanded by sense or feeling.

3 There is more rhythmical freedom.

Together, these technical advantages can assist the skilled poet to achieve a fusion between the patterns of sound and sense. This was especially important to Milton who strove constantly for an almost overwhelming concentration of meaning and feeling. Jonathan Richardson commented:

> *A Reader of Milton must be always upon Duty; he is surrounded with Sense, it rises in every Line, every Word is to the purpose; there are no Lazy Intervals, All has been Consider'd, and Demands and Merits Observation. Even in the Best Writers you Sometimes find Words and Sentences which hang on so Loosely you may Blow 'em Off; Milton's are all Substance and Weight; Fewer would not have Served the Turn, and More would have been Superfluous.*[18]

It is a commonplace that Milton devised a syntax of his own that stems from Latin even more than normal English. There follow now some notes on this special style which suggest why it seemed necessary for his purposes.

ORATORY AND INVECTIVE

The experience of polemic that Milton acquired in his writings on behalf of the Commonwealth was not wasted in *Paradise Lost*. See the exchange of insults between Satan and Gabriel towards the end of Book IV. Here is Gabriel:

> *And thou sly hypocrit, who now wouldst seem*
> *Patron of liberty, who more then thou*
> *Once fawnd, and cring'd, and servilly ador'd*
> *Heav'ns awful Monarch? wherefore but in hope*
> *To dispossess him, and thy self to reigne?*[19]

Notice how Milton is able to place 'Patron' at the beginning of a line. Try, noting the commas, the sound effect of:

Once fawnd, and cring'd, and servilly ador'd.

Consider how the structure of the final line and a half enables Milton to finish the line on the strong word 'reigne'.

It is a similar skill that informs the grim humour of the Paradise of Fools. The inhabitants of this Limbo think themselves at the gates of Heaven itself:

when loe
A violent cross wind from either Coast
Blows them transverse ten thousand Leagues awry
Into the devious Air; then might ye see
Cowles, Hoods and Habits with thir wearers tost
And flutterd into Raggs, then Reliques, Beads,
Indulgences, Dispenses, Pardons, Bulls,
The sport of Winds: all these upwhirld aloft
Fly ore the backside of the World farr off
Into a Limbo *large and broad.*[20]

The structure here is more direct than usual, as is needed.

MILTON'S SYNTAX

Look at these examples:

1 Satan finally forces his way through the conflicting elements of Chaos:

But glad that now his Sea should find a shore,
With fresh alacritie and force renewd
Springs upward like a Pyramid of fire
Into the wild expanse, and through the shock
Of fighting Elements, on all sides round
Environd wins his way; harder beset
And more endangerd, then when Argo *passd*
Through Bosporus *betwixt the justling Rocks:*
Or when Ulysses *on the Larbord shunnd*
Charybdis, *and by th'other whirlpool steard.*
So hee with difficulty and labour hard
Mov'd on, with difficulty and labour hee.[21]

i Notice the placing and the force of 'Springs'. The word is in the middle of the upward movement and marks a fresh impetus

ii To balance 'Springs' at the beginning of a line is 'shock at the end of the next. The pace slows down here.

iii Again, note the placing of 'environd' at the beginning of the line.

iv What is the effect of the two parallel classical analogies? Firstly, both refer to long and dangerous voyages. Both analogies are to especially difficult and perilous feats of seamanship.

v The repetition of the two final lines of the paragraph almost re-enact in their movement the painful and arduous success of Satan. Note how the syntax allows Milton to end the line with 'hee'.

This passage is from Book I, 1011–22, and prepares the way for the following lines which tell us of the easy route from hell to earth after the Fall. Milton's use of the resources of his blank verse to convey in sound patterns a sense of Satan's struggle is not only there for its own sake. It exists to strengthen the contrast. How easy is it for Sin and Death now!

2 At the end of Book IV the Archangel Gabriel has the last word in a debate with Satan. He shews the Fiend the golden scales of God in whose justice Satan weighs not at all:

> Satan, *I know thy strength, and thou knowst mine,*
> *Neither our own but giv'n; what follie then*
> *To boast what arms can doe, since thine no more*
> *Than Heav'n permits, nor mine, though doubl'd now*
> *To trample thee as mire: for proof look up,*
> *And read thy Lot in yon celestial Sign*
> *Where thou art weighd, and shown how light, how weak,*
> *If thou resist. The Fiend lookd up and knew*
> *His mounted scale aloft: nor more; but fled*
> *Murmuring, and with him fled the shades of night.*[22]

i The phrase at the beginning of the second line is very condensed. Presumably it means: Our strength is not our own but was given us (by God). Milton's syntax places the stress on 'giv'n' with its following pause.

ii The next three lines have a very complicated structure. A paraphrase might be: 'How foolish it is of you to boast what you might do by arms since your power is no more than allowed you by Heaven. My power, too, comes from Heaven though I have double strength given me to trample you into the mud.' It is not just that any paraphrase *must* be longer but that the Miltonic structure permits, in his blank verse, the placing of stress on the key words: follie, boast, Heav'n, doubl'd, trample, mire. In particular, the sentence balances round the word Heav'n. It begins with 'follie' and it ends with 'mire'.

iii Notice how effective is the inversion (or delay) of 'murmuring' so it starts a line.

3 Much of the effect of *Paradise Lost* comes from contrast—good and evil, delight and woe. A further marked feature of the

poem is the way Milton keeps, as we have stressed before, Heaven and Hell, past and future simultaneously before our minds. I am indebted for the following example to Winifred Nowottny (from her remarkable book: *The Language Poets Use*, Athlone Press, 1962). Lucifer has unfurled his rebellious banner in Heaven. Only the Angel Abdiel remains loyal to God in the rebel camp. He warns Satan, before his departure, of the retribution of God. In so doing, he must encompass in his speech a sense of what the rebellion means, its predictable failure in the end, the immediate consequences (the fires of hell) and the omnipotence of God. And all this has to be said in a *dramatic* setting. Blank verse line and grammar need the most careful construction to contain such meaning and such feeling. Notice how it is done:

for soon expect to feel
His Thunder on thy head, devouring fire.
Then who created thee lamenting learne,
When who can uncreate thee thou shalt know.[23]

i Thunder is to be expected; there are Biblical references, as well as the commonplaces of classical legend (thunderbolts of Jove).

ii Note the matching of 'devouring' and 'lamenting'. Note also the alliteration of 'lamenting learne'. Further 'learne' at the end of one line is set against 'knowe' at the end of the next.

iii 'Then' . . . 'When'. 'created' . . . 'uncreate'. The grammar strongly reinforces the contrast.

The point is that the unfamiliar syntax used by Milton gave him, at best, a remarkable freedom to get individual words into exactly the right place for emphasis and in relation to one another.

Here are two further examples. Both are famous passages. Eve has just eaten the forbidden fruit:

So saying, her rash hand in evil hour
Forth reaching to the Fruit, she pluckd, she eat:
Earth felt the wound, and Nature from her seat
Sighing through all her Works gave signs of woe
That all was lost.[24]

Notice how much is gained from being able to use the tighter construction at the start—the two participles 'saying' and 'reaching'. What would be the standard English way of making the same point? Notice, too, the way the proper stress comes on the key final word—'lost'.

26. *Apollo and Daphne* by Bernini in the Borghese Gallery, Rome (The Mansell Collection)

The second example is in Book X. Satan returns to Hell in triumph. But appropriate retribution reaches him even here. We have already compared Milton's descriptive effect in words with Bernini's statue of Apollo and Daphne metamorphosed into a tree:

So having said, a while he stood, expecting
Thir universal shout and high applause
To fill his eare, when contrary he hears
On all sides, from innumerable tongues
A dismal universal hiss, the sound
Of public scorn; he wonderd, but not long
Had leasure, wondring at himself now more;
His Visage drawn he felt to sharp and spare,
His Armes clung to his Ribs, his Leggs entwining
Each other, till supplanted down he fell
A monstrous Serpent on his Belly prone,
Reluctant, but in vaine: a greater power
Now rul'd him, punisht in the shape he sinnd,
According to his doom.[25]

This needs to be read carefully aloud to see how the words and falling rhythm and repeated 's' sounds bring us to 'scorn'. Then mark how the movement of the verse almost re-enacts the metamorphosis leading to the key words in which Milton makes his point, linking the change back to the temptation of Eve and forward to Satan's final doom. Notice especially the placing of the monosyllables: prone, vaine, doom.

OTHER FEATURES

1 Milton, exploiting his classical knowledge, often uses English words of classical derivation in such a way that both the English meaning and the original Latin sense are present. For example, in 'ere he arrive the happy Isle' he may well have had in mind the original Latin 'come to shore'. Certainly in 'sagacious of his quarry from so far', he is using the Latin sense 'acutely discerning'. There is a pun in the following:

who shall tempt with wandring feet
The dark unbottomd infinite Abyss,
And through the palpable obscure find out
His uncouth way.[26]

The original meaning of 'uncouth' is 'unknown'—but the way surely was rough! There are many such exploitations of older meanings and such puns.

2 Milton is famous for his extended similes. These are often historic or legendary parallels. Sometimes they are taken from the experiences of travellers or ancient beliefs about natural phenomena. What is the impact of such a simile? Is it a digression? Does it help us to visualize a scene? Such similes are especially common when Milton is narrating the Satanic drama. Do they help to place a narrative moment in that wider context of which Milton constantly wishes us to be aware?

3 We saw earlier that Milton could at times be over-conscious of his meaning and neglect its embodiment. The description of Sin suggests he was thinking more about the interpretation of the allegory than of getting the picture into focus. It is said that Coleridge could not sleep when this (from Book XI) was pointed out to him:

Sight so deform what heart of Rock could long
Drie-ey'd behold'.[27]

In Book V, the Eternal Eye (God) sees all but also (seven lines later) smiles and talks!

THE POETRY

Milton was blind, living in an England that had deserted the Good Old Cause when he wrote his three final great poems. Samson, the national hero, ended his days in loneliness, betrayed to his political enemies, blinded. It was in the marriage bed that Samson told Delilah the secret of his strength which led to her betrayal of him. The despair of Samson and the struggle to regain strength and purpose are very close to Milton's own experience.

So vertue giv'n for lost
Deprest, and overthrown, as seemd,
Like that self-begott'n bird
In the Arabian woods embost,
That no second knows nor third,
And lay erewhile a Holocaust,
From out her ashie womb now teemd
Revives, reflourishes, then vigorous most
When most unactive deemd,
And though her body die, her fame survives,[28]

In the end, the verse itself has become plain and spare, almost simple. Samson, says Milton, has given his servants fresh understanding 'of true experience from this great event'. In *Paradise Regained*, Christ is to conquer over Sin and Death by 'strong Sufferance'.

These are reminders that we read the poetry for its effect as a *whole*, for the sum more than the parts, for the message, no doubt, but also for the man.

[1] Milton 'On the Death of a Fair Infant' [2] Milton *On Time* (1629) [3] Spenser *Shepheardes Calender* [4] Milton 'L'Allegro' [5] Spenser *Shepheards Calender* [6] Milton 'Lycidas' [7] Milton *Comus* [8] *Paradise Lost* V, 291–7 [9] John Donne 'The Good-Morrow' [10] John Donne 'Holy Sonnet XIV' [11] Richard Crashaw 'An Hymn of the Nativity' [12] Milton 'Ode on the Morning of Christ's Nativity' [13] Milton 'Lycidas' [14] Milton *Comus* 331–5 [15] *ibid.* 710–20 [16] *ibid.* 46–53 [17] Milton, Preface to *Paradise Lost* [18] Jonathan Richardson *Early Lives* (1734) [19] *Paradise Lost* IV, 957–61 [20] *ibid.* III, 442–97 [21] *ibid.* I, 1011–22 [22] *ibid.* IV, 1006–15 [23] *ibid.* V, 892–5 [24] *ibid.* IX, 780–84 [25] *ibid.* X, 504–17 [26] *ibid.* II, 404–7 [27] *ibid.* XI, 494–5 [28] Milton *Samson Agonistes* 1697–1706

9

Editing Milton

A lot can go wrong when producing a book; it is surprising that so little does. In the seventeenth century, the author was usually at the mercy of his printer (who was also publisher). The printer depended on the handwritten manuscript of his author. The printed text could differ in a number of particulars from what an author actually wrote. Errors could be compounded in second and subsequent editions.

Further, English spelling and punctuation was not uniform in Milton's time. It was not unusual for a printer to impose his own house style upon an author. A good printer would do this job well; a less competent printer could produce a text of uncertain sense—a problem for editors in later generations.

Surprisingly, though, there are not many problems of this kind with John Milton. The first collected edition of his poems was published in 1645 and he had a good printer. As we shall see, he allowed his printer some liberty in this volume with spelling and punctuation. In addition, a modern editor has a check of remarkable value. Trinity College in Cambridge possesses a manuscript of some of these poems in Milton's hand with his own alterations and corrections. The manuscript shows the poet at work; it also suggests to the modern editor how Milton might have wanted his poems to appear on the printed page.

Paradise Lost was, of course, written when Milton was blind. He had to employ scribes to take down dictation. One might think that the chances for error would have been much greater. In fact, Milton was himself a most precise and careful editor of his own work. The first edition appeared in the August of 1667. There was a second edition in July 1674 and this was revised personally by Milton. In spite of his blindness, he was able to insist on supervising every detail. First of all, he dictated passages to his scribes. They then corrected what they had written after they had read it back to him, no doubt more than once.

He was then very careful about correcting the proofs sent him by his printer. After the first edition came out, he discovered a number of errors and subsequent impressions were accompanied by a page of *errata*. Finally, he thoroughly revised his text for the 1674 edition. It is a text based on this edition that has been used for quotations from *Paradise Lost* in this book (*The Poetical Works of John Milton*, Ed. H. Darbyshire (O.U.P., 1958)).

Because of his own poetic nature, because of the importance to him of the speaking aloud of his verses, Milton was especially

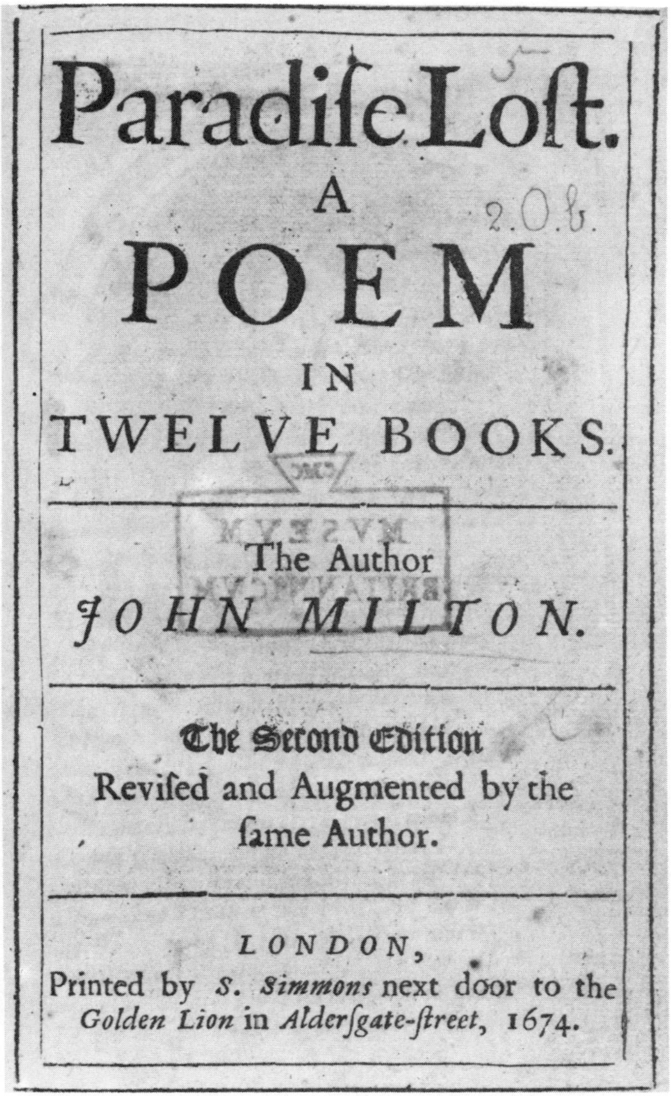

Paradiſe Loſt.

A

POEM

IN

TWELVE BOOKS.

The Author

JOHN MILTON.

The Second Edition

Reviſed and Augmented by the ſame Author.

LONDON,

Printed by *S. Simmons* next door to the *Golden Lion* in *Alderſgate-ſtreet*, 1674.

27. The title page of the Second Edtion of *Paradise Lost*, 1674 (British Library Board)

anxious that the printed text should indicate as clearly as possible how the poem should be read aloud. To make these intentions clear, he developed a system both of spelling and punctuation. Here is the beginning of Beelzebub's speech in Book I:

O Prince, O Chief of many Throned Powers,
That led th'imbatteld Seraphim to Warr
Under thy conduct, and in dreadful deeds
Fearless, endangerd Heav'ns perpetual King;
And put to proof his high Supremacy,
Whether upheld by strength, or Chance, or Fate;
Too well I see and rue the dire event,
That with sad overthrow and foul defeat
Hath lost us Heav'n.[1]

It reveals many of his principles:

1 The spelling makes the pronunciation clear—especially when it is a matter of one or two syllables. So *Heav'n* is *one* syllable. When Milton needed the word to be disyllabic, he had it spelt *Heaven*.

2 Similarly, he always marked elisions as in 'th'imbattld Seraphim'. Notice the spelling of *imbatteld* and *endangerd*.

3 He distinguished in spelling a verb in the past tense from its past participle:

So spake th'Apostat Angel, though in pain,
Vaunting loud, but rackt with deep despair:
And him thus answerd soon his bold Compeer.

Rackt is a past participle, a verbal adjective. *Answerd* is the ordinary past tense of the verb.

4 He marked emphatic from unemphatic forms of pronouns: we, me, ye—wee, mee, yee. There is a similar distinction between thir and their. So:

Be it so, since hee
Who now is Sovran can dispose and bid
What shall be right:

5 Compare:

Whom reason hath eqald, force hath made supream

where the accent is on the second syllable, with

And sat as Princes, whom the supreme *King*

where it is on the first syllable.

6 Milton also made careful distinction between words of similar pronunciation but different meaning. For example we find counsell (verb) and councell (noun), foul and fowl.

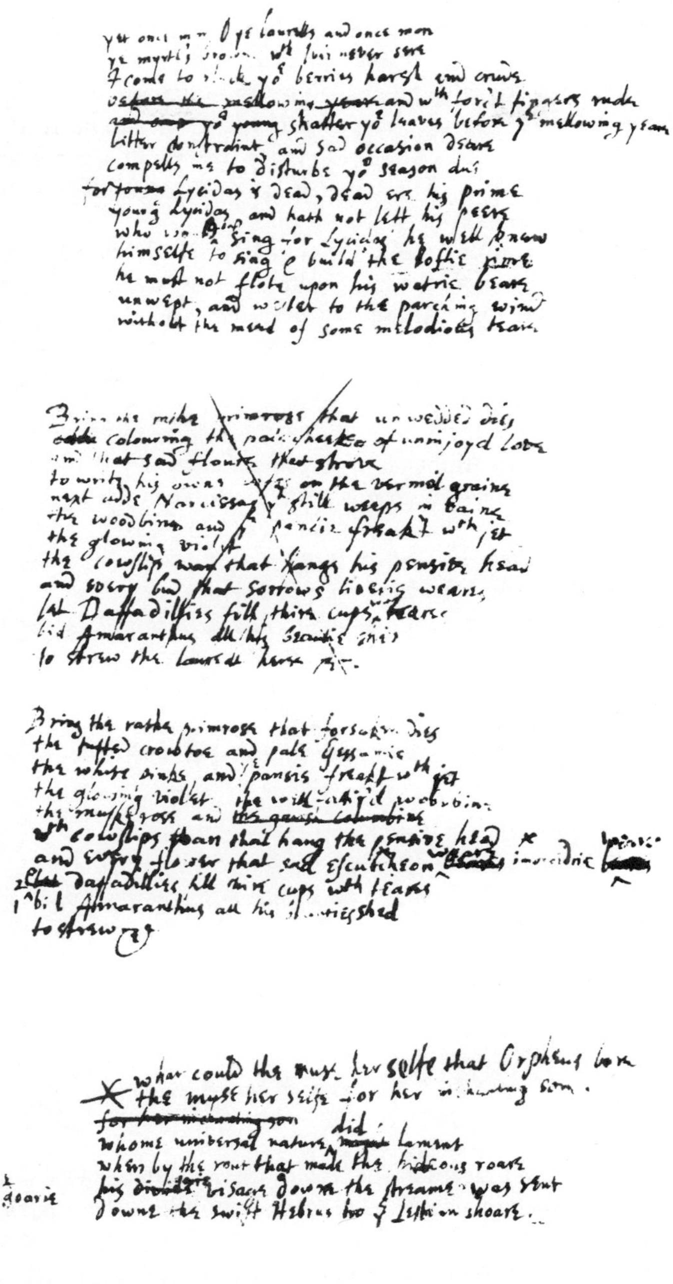

28. A page from Milton's MS. of 'Lycidas' in Trinity College Library (Cambridge University Library)

Milton had, of course, a number of favoured spellings of his own. He retained a number of older English forms such as 'farder' for farther and 'hunderd' for hundred. The latter makes a point about pronunciation as well.

Milton was equally precise about punctuation. His long paragraphs needed very careful punctuation to assist the reader. For example, he used the full stop to mark the end of a paragraph and to introduce speech. The colon is used to mark off independent sections in a paragraph.

Editorial troubles came after Milton's death. Nineteenth-century editors, in particular, could not leave well alone. They did not understand that Milton had a system and they corrected his spelling and his punctuation quite mercilessly. Here are some lines from 'Lycidas', first, as in the 1645 edition, and, second, as in the nineteenth-century Palgrave's Golden Treasury.

1 *Return* Alpheus, *the dread voice is past,*
That shrunk thy streams; Return Sicilian *Muse,*
And call the Vales, and bid them hither cast
Their Bels, and Flourets of a thousand hues.
Ye valleys low where the milde whispers use,
Of shades and wanton winds, and gushing brooks,
On whose fresh lap the swart Star sparely looks,
Throw hither all your quaint enameld eyes,
That on the green terf suck the honied showres,
And purple all the ground with vernal flowres.[2]

2 *Return Alpheus; the dread voice is past*
That shrunk thy streams; return, Sicilian Muse,
And call the vales, and bid them hither cast
Their bells and flowerets of a thousand hues.
Ye valleys low, where the mild whispers use
Of shades, and wanton winds, and gushing brooks
On whose fresh lap the swart star sparely looks;
Throw hither all your quaint enamell'd eyes
That on the green turf suck the honey'd showers
And purple all the ground with vernal flowers.[2]

Compare the two carefully. Do the modern spellings ever interfere with what Milton intended? Note, carefully, the changes in punctuation. Test the differences by reading aloud. Clearly, Milton's own version does present difficulties to the modern reader who is no specialist in the period. How far can a modern editor of a popular poetry book go without damage to the original?

Here now are the opening lines to Book III of *Paradise Lost* firstly from Milton's second edition and, secondly, from an early twentieth-century cheap edition (Everyman) based on the work of a nineteenth-century editor, David Masson. Again, compare the two and note the effect of Masson's changes.

1 *Hail holy Light, ofspring of Heav'n first-born,*
Or of th'Eternal Coeternal beam
May I express thee unblam'd? since God is Light,
And never but in unapproached Light
Dwelt from Eternitie, dwelt then in thee,
Bright effluence of bright essence increate.
Or hear'st thou rather pure Ethereal stream,
Whose Fountain who shall tell? before the Sun
Before the Heav'ns thou wert, and at the voice
Of God, as with a Mantle didst invest
The rising world of waters dark and deep,
Won from the void and formless infinite.[3]

2 *Hail, holy Light, offspring of Heaven first-born!*
Or of the Eternal coeternal beam
May I express thee unblamed? since God is light,
And never but in unapproachèd light
Dwelt from eternity—dwelt then in thee,
Bright effluence of bright essence increate!
Or hear'st thou rather pure Ethereal stream,
Whose fountain who shall tell? Before the Sun,
Before the Heavens, thou wert, and at the voice
Of God, as with a mantle, didst invest
The rising World of waters dark and deep,
Won from the void and formless Infinite![3]

[1] *Paradise Lost* I, 128–36 [2] Milton 'Lycidas' 132–41 [3] *Paradise Lost* III, 1–12

10

The Influence of Milton

Restoration England was not Milton's England and the fashionable writers of the time hardly knew what to make of him. His poetry had little in common with the rhymed couplets of satire and moralistic reflection or with the declamatory posturings that the theatre took for tragedy. Dryden, who was the accepted leader of literary taste, recognized his greatness and even paid him a visit—to suggest making an opera out of *Paradise Lost*. The major poems sold well, better than Shakespeare, in fact, but Shakespeare was also out of fashion. There was a puritan readership for Milton, even if he was little considered in court circles.

There had to be a change in the social and political climate before the reading public could properly absorb Milton. The Restoration period was too politically violent, too concerned with the old fears of Catholicism and old country resentments of city business for an author of revolutionary tracts to be *generally* accepted.

When Milton was accepted he was accepted, like any major author, in the likeness of the age which made him its own. It was a series of essays by Addison in his periodical, *The Spectator*, that established Milton's critical respectability. *The Spectator* was a very influential journal which took London, respectably attired, to the provinces. Addison praised Milton for his *classical* qualities; he became a figure, rather larger than life and of the past. When Addison was writing, there were many people still alive who had known Milton. There were men involved in religion and politics who had felt the force of commitment to the 'Good Old Cause'. Yet Addison's Milton was placed, for the readers of *The Spectator*, beyond this kind of controversy.

> *Milton . . . by the choice of the noblest words and phrases which our tongue would afford him, has carried our language to a greater height than any of the English poets have ever done before or after him, and made the* sublimity (my emphasis) *of his style equal to that of his sentiments.*[1]

Milton was beyond criticism now but notice that he was to be read for the elevation of his sentiments. A reader of *Paradise Lost* was to be transported beyond earthly things to be improved by noble language and by noble thoughts.

The most distinguished poet of early eighteenth-century England was Alexander Pope. He was, among other things, a satirist. He accepted Addison's judgment and, in particular, felt Milton not to be modern. Sublimity was fine in the classics but a much easier style was needed for treating of the contemporary world. So Pope used Milton in two different ways in his own writings. There are strong echoes in his translation of epic Homer. Then there are deliberately deflationary uses of Milton in his satirical poems. Pope specialized in the mock epic where a comical grandeur of style exposed the pretensions of the petty. In Book IV of the *Dunciad*, he opens with a mock invocation. The Goddess of Dulness is to take her throne:

Yet, yet a moment, one dim ray of light
Indulge, dread Chaos, and eternal Night!
Of darkness visible so much be lent,
As half to show, half veil the deep intent.
Ye pow'rs! whose mysteries restored I sing,
To whom Time bears me on his rapid wing,
Suspend a while your force inertly strong,
Then take at once the poet and the song.[2]

The style is borrowed and there is even direct quotation ('darkness visible').

Pope, as great poets do, could use other poets in his own writing. The eighteenth-century emphasis on Milton's style tended to shackle the lesser talents. Miltonic style was thought to be appropriate for any subject. Here is Dyer discussing the textile trade:

Ingenious trade, to clothe the naked world,
Her soft materials, not from sheep alone,
From various animals, reeds, trees, and stones,
Collects sagacious; in Euboea's isle
A wondrous rock is found, of which are woven
Vests incombustible: Batavia, flax;
Siam's warm marish yields the fissile cane;
Soft Persia, silk; Balasor's shady hills,
Tough bark of trees; Peruvian Pito, grass;
And every sultry clime the snowy down

Of cotton, bursting from its stubborn shell
To gleam amid the verdure of the grove.[3]

This may be the only reference in English verse to asbestos but the passage also shows very clearly two ways in which the example of Milton dominated verse writing. The Latinate syntax is there. Secondly, we can see what came to be called 'poetic diction'. The pastoral tradition remained in the eighteenth century; it was very much part of the classical tradition. With it went what one might almost call a standard list of acceptable epithets and descriptions. In Milton we see the style in his descriptions of the Garden of Eden. Eden had to be credible yet of the art of God not man:

Thus was this place,
A happy rural seat of various view;
Groves whose rich Trees wept odorous Gumms and Balme,
Others whose fruit burnisht with Gold'n Rinde
Hung amiable, Hesperian *Fables true,*
If true, here onely, and of delicious taste:
Betwixt them Lawns, or level Downs, and Flocks
Grasing the tender herb, were interpos'd,
Of palmie hilloc, or the flourie lap
Of som irriguous Valley spred her store,
Flours of all hue, and without Thorn the Rose:
Another side, umbrageous Grots and Caves.[4]

and so on. This is some remove from any real landscape; it is perhaps art describing art. Here, now, is a gentle country poet, William Cowper (1731–1800):

See Nature gay as when she first began,
With smiles alluring her admirer, man;
She spreads the morning over eastern hills;
Earth glitters with the drops the night distils;
The sun obedient at her call appears,
To fling his glories o'er the robe she wears;
Banks clothed with flowers, groves filled with sprightly sounds,
The yellow tilth, green meads, rocks, rising grounds,
Streams edged with osiers, fattening every field
Where'er they flow, now seen and now concealed;[5]

It is not that Cowper has not used his eyes. What he sees reaches the page in conventional phraseology. He writes in the shadow of Addison's Milton.

THE ROMANTIC MILTON

In the *Lyrical Ballads*, Wordsworth consciously broke away from the pseudo-Miltonic poetic diction and sought poetry in the language of ordinary country folk. He was the prophet and the herald of the Romantic Movement. It was a literature of change; it was a literature of individualism. It celebrated the struggle of the single man to make his life. The Romantic hero or heroine sought to cast off the chains of the past, to become more fully himself or herself.

The Romantics found a different Milton. Shelley saluted the old revolutionary:

> *the sacred Milton was, let it ever be remembered, a republican, and a bold enquirer into morals and religion. The great writers of our own age are, we have reason to suppose, the companions and forerunners of some unimagined change in our social condition or the opinions which cement it.*[6]

The Romantics were interested in the *characters* of *Paradise Lost*. Especially were they interested in Milton's Satan. He was a tragic figure; he was the archetypal rebel, the great individualist; he was also evil, a tyrant. So in Byron:

> *There was in him a vital scorn of all:*
> *As if the worst had fallen which could befall,*
> *He stood a stranger in this breathing world,*
> *An erring spirit from another hurled.*[7]

The hero/villain who defies God or morality is a popular figure not only in Romantic poetry but also in the novel. The paperback section of a railway bookstall will reveal contemporary examples. Satan as both tyrant and victim has excited many imaginations. What a great artist can make of the Satanic, mediated through Byron and the Gothic novelists such as Mary Shelley, can be seen in Emily Brontë's *Wuthering Heights*. In her introduction to the novel, Charlotte Brontë talks of Heathcliff's soul:

> *the ever-suffering soul of a magnate of the infernal world: and by its quenchless and ceaseless ravage effect the execution of the decree which dooms him to carry Hell with him wherever he wanders.*[8]

So Satan when he reaches earth and views Paradise for the first time:

horror and doubt distract
His troubl'd thoughts, and from the bottom stirr
The Hell within him, for within him Hell
He brings, and round about him, nor from Hell
One step no more then from himself can fly
By change of place.[9]

Romantic writers found, then, in Milton deep echoes of their own preoccupations. The most profound and the most radical re-interpretation of Milton came from William Blake (1757–1827). Not only did he illustrate Milton—the example here shows God judging Adam and there is another example on page 75—but he constantly rewrote the theme of *Paradise Lost* in his own poems. To Blake, evil was what he called Reason (and Newton was its prophet). Reason imprisoned the soul of man and caged his

29. *God Judging Adam* by William Blake, 1795 (Reproduced by permission of the Trustees of the Tate Gallery, London)

creative energies. Man is most godlike, most himself when he is the revolutionary, the prophet of *love*. To Blake, the God of the traditional Christianity, the God of Milton's poem, was Satan:

> *Thy purpose & the purpose of thy Priests & of thy Churches*
> *Is to impress on men the fear of death, to teach*
> *Trembling & fear, terror, constriction, abject selfishness*[10]

And in the Satan of *Paradise Lost* Blake saw the divine energy:

> *Note: The reason Milton wrote in fetters when he wrote of Angels & God, and at liberty when of Devils & Hell, is because he was a true Poet and of the Devil's party without knowing it.*[11]

The final line of *The Marriage of Heaven & Hell* is:

> '*For every thing that lives is Holy.*'

NINETEENTH CENTURY AND AFTER

Respectability returned to Milton in the Victorian period. He had become something of a national monument. The Satanic hero/villain was not central to Victorian taste, in spite of writers like Poe. The Romantic rejection of Miltonic style meant that he was not much of a writer's quarry. There were few signs of the kind of struggle that Keats had with Miltonic epic when searching for an individual voice for his *Hyperion*. Milton had become academic. There are suggestions in Victorian writers that they found him too removed from human concerns. His concerns seemed little relevant to theirs in an age of material prosperity for the middle classes and of spiritual doubt.

There were many cheap reprints, however. There are signs that Milton was much read by working men. The Chartist, Thomas Cooper, found an education in Milton. His prose writings were an encouragement to those concerned with the extension of civil liberties.

Milton's reputation has suffered rather more this century for two main reasons. Many poets and literary critics have found his writing at an opposite pole to their own. Many poets have sought the cadences of ordinary speech and derived their imagery from daily life. He has not offered the metaphorical depth and particularity of Shakespeare nor that curious amalgam of intellect and passion our age has found in the metaphysicals.

30. *The Fallen Angels*, in the suburbs of Hell while their peers consult in Pandemonium, by John Martin, 1841, an example of Victorian engineering meeting Milton. John Martin's imagination was kindled by the *vastness* of Milton's cosmos—a scale which to him linked it with contemporary technology (Reproduced by permission of the Trustees of the Tate Gallery, London)

Secondly, we continue to live in the Romantic epoch. Writers, at almost all levels, have been concerned with the inner man, with individual self-fulfilment, with the search for 'identity'. We have 'supp'd full of horrors' and have turned to violence or to love (or both) as routes from our predicaments. Yet we have had to face the irrational power of Hitler and we still do not know how to control greed, envy and pride. The assurance and the will of a John Milton can seem very alien. He lacked guilt as we know it and where is there room in our small bickering world for the sublime? Robert Graves found him an arrogant prig and there often seems a kind of antique desperation in those academics who defend him.

Milton remains, though, a liberating force. He *compels* his readers to lift their faces from the ground and grapple with larger perspectives. He is a discoverer and he went wherever his intellectual will drove him, whatever the cost.

> *Well knows he who uses to consider, that our faith and knowledge thrives by exercise, as well as our limbs and*

complexion. Truth is compared in Scripture to a streaming fountain: if her waters flow not in a perpetual progression, they sicken into a muddy pool of conformity and tradition. . . . Let her and Falsehood grapple; who ever knew Truth put to the worse, in a free and open encounter.[12]

Milton remains; each age can find from him what it needs or, at times, what it must reject. The Paradise was Milton's and he created God, Satan, Adam and Eve. And so do we; we find our own good and evil and we learn how to make the best of unattained ideals:

Death and life were not
Till man made up the whole,
Made lock, stock and barrel
Out of his bitter soul,
Aye, sun and moon and star, all.[13]

[1] Addison *The Spectator* [2] Alexander Pope *The Dunciad* IV, 1–8 [3] John Dyer 'The Fleece' (1757) [4] *Paradise Lost* IV, 246–57 [5] William Cowper 'Hope' [6] Percy Bysshe Shelley, Preface to *Prometheus Unbound* [7] Lord Byron *Lara* (1814) [8] Charlotte Brontë, Introduction to *Wuthering Heights* [9] *Paradise Lost* IV, 18–23 [10] William Blake *Milton* Book 2 Stanza 43 [11] William Blake *Marriage of Heaven and Hell* [12] Milton *Areopagitica* (1644) [13] W. B. Yeats 'The Tower'

Chronology

REIGN OF JAMES I 1603–25		
1608	Birth of Milton	
1609		Shakespeare's *Sonnets* published
1611		Authorised Version of the Bible
1616	Attends St Paul's School	Voyage of *Mayflower*
1620		Death of Shakespeare
REIGN OF CHARLES I 1625–49		
1625	Christ's College, Cambridge	
1628	*Vacation Exercise*	
1629	Graduates B.A. 'Nativity Ode'	Parliament dissolved. Charles rules alone
1630	*Arcades* (?), *The Passion* *On Shakespeare*	
1631	'L'Allegro' and 'Il Penseroso'	
1632	M.A. Father retires to Hammersmith where Milton studies	
1634	*Comus* performed at Ludlow Castle, 29th September	
1635	Continues studies at Horton, Bucks	
1638	'Lycidas' published Visit to France and Italy	
1639	Return to London Teacher	First Bishops' War
1640		Short Parliament. Beginning of Long Parliament. Strafford and Laud impeached. Death of Rubens
1641	Pamphlets about Bishops	Grand Remonstrance
1642	Married Mary Powell *Reasons of Church Government* *Apology for Smectymnuus*	Civil War begins
1643	Divorce pamphlet	
1644	*Areopagitica*	Marston Moor
1645	Mary returns. Larger house in Barbican *Collected Poems*	Book of Common Prayer abolished Naseby
1647	Death of father	

COMMONWEALTH 1649–60

1649	*On the Tenure of Kings and Magistrates* Appointed Secretary for Foreign Tongues	Trial and execution of Charles I
1651	*Defensio Pro Populo Anglicano*	
1652	Becomes totally blind Death of wife, Mary	
1653		Cromwell, Lord Protector
1654	*Defensio Secunda*	
1656	Marries Katherine Woodcock Begins writing *Christian Doctrine*	
1658	Katherine and daughter die Begins writing *Paradise Lost*	Death of Cromwell
1660	*A Ready and Easy Way to Establish a Free Commonwealth*	Restoration

REIGN OF CHARLES II 1660–85

1663	Marries Elizabeth Minshull	
1665	Chalfont St Giles because of plague	
1666		Fire of London
1667	*Paradise Lost* published	
1670	*History of Britain*	
1671	*Paradise Regained* and *Samson Agonistes* published	
1673	Dryden visits Milton to ask about making opera of *Paradise Lost* 2nd Edition of *Poems*	
1674	2nd Edition of *Paradise Lost* Died 8th November	

Bibliography

LIFE

HANFORD, J. H. *John Milton, Englishman* (Gollancz, 1950) Short and readable

GRAVES, ROBERT *Wife to Mr Milton* (Cassell, 1943; Portway reprint, 1969) Brilliant and very unfair, but good for background

HISTORY

ASHLEY, MAURICE *England in the Seventeenth Century* (Pelican History of England Vol. 6, 3rd edition 1961)

PRALL, STUART (Ed.) *The Puritan Revolution*—A Documentary History (Routledge & Kegan Paul, 1969) A valuable background collection

WEDGWOOD, C. V. *The King's Peace* (Collins, 1955; Fontana, 1966) and *The King's War* (Collins, 1958; Fontana, 1966) Well-researched and vivid accounts from a Royalist standpoint

HILL, CHRISTOPHER *Reformation to Industrial Revolution* (Weidenfeld & Nicolson, 1967; Pelican, 1969) Social and economic background to revolution

HILL, CHRISTOPHER *The World Turned Upside Down* (M. T. Smith, 1972; Pelican, 1975) A fascinating study of radical ideas showing, inter alia, Milton's links

BACKGROUND

WILSON, JOHN DOVER (Ed.) *Life in Shakespeare's England* (Penguin, 1968) Some of the material in this classic helps understanding of the world and the London into which Milton was born

GARDNER, HELEN (Ed.) *The Metaphysical Poets* (O.U.P., 1957; Penguin, 1969) A useful selection of other poetry of Milton's day

GRIERSON, H. J. C. (Ed.) *Metaphysical Lyrics and Poems of the Seventeenth Century* (O.U.P., 1965) Originally published in 1921, this remains deservedly the most comprehensive anthology of Caroline schools of poetry

MURRAY, LINDA *The Late Renaissance and Mannerism* (1967)

SEWTER, A. C. *Baroque and Rococo Art* (1972)
The above are two of several useful volumes of art history published by Thames and Hudson

TILLYARD, E. M. W. *The Elizabethan World Picture* (Chatto & Windus, 1943; Penguin, 1972) and *The Miltonic Setting* (Chatto & Windus, 1938) For scholasticism, Elizabethan concepts of the universe and seventeenth-century science but most good editions of Milton also contain such material

BROADBENT, JOHN (Ed.) *John Milton—Introductions* (O.U.P., 1973) Designed for university use but 'A' Level students could find it helpful especially on the Bible, art and music

WILLEY, BASIL *The Seventeenth Century Background* (Chatto & Windus, 1934; Penguin 1972) For those who develop an interest in the philosophical background

CRITICISM

Any list must select from the very large number of books that have been published about Milton. The following are fairly accessible, not too abstruse and represent a number of different viewpoints about Milton.

RALEIGH, WALTER *Milton* (Ed. Arnold, 1909) If this can be found in a library or secondhand, it is worth reading both for its clarity and its useful comments on Milton's style

TILLYARD, E. M. W. *Milton* (British Council, 1930; Penguin, 1968) Perhaps not very critical but a good solid and readable account of the man and his work

LEAVIS, F. R. *Revaluation* (Chatto & Windus, 1936; Penguin, 1972) A classic of literary criticism. His essay on Milton's 'dislodgement' contains the central modern attack on Milton's style—its un-English, Latinate and essentially lifeless quality

WALDOCK, A. J. A. *Paradise Lost and Its Critics* (O.U.P., 1947) Much praised by Leavis. Waldock analyses what he considers to be the inconsistencies and structural weaknesses of the epic, treating it perhaps as if it were a novel

KERMODE, FRANK (Ed.) *The Living Milton* (Routledge & Kegan Paul, 1960) Essays partly in answer to Waldock but mainly concerned with establishing positive responses to Milton. There is some vigorous and effective critical writing

PATRIDES, C. A. (Ed.) *Milton's Epic Poetry* (Penguin, 1967) A useful collection of papers which show something of contemporary thinking about the great poems

Audio-Visual Material

The National Committee for Audio-Visual Aids in Education publish a series of multi-media kits to link with *Authors in Their Age*, consisting of filmstrip, cassette and notes. The Milton one has two main themes—Milton and Europe and the way he has been seen by later generations. Full details from 33 Queen Anne Street, London W1M 0AL.

To See

The National Gallery, London has many examples of Mannerist and Baroque art.

There are still extant examples of architecture contemporary with Milton. See, for example, Inigo Jones's Banqueting Hall in Whitehall. The Great Fire of 1666 and the Second World War destroyed the seventeenth-century city, so one can get more of the feel of town life of the period in towns outside London. The colleges at Cambridge can be visited and Christ's College looks much as it did.

The magnificent Wren Library at Trinity College, Cambridge contains a priceless Milton MS. with corrected drafts of such early works as *Comus* and 'Lycidas'.

The cottage at Chalfont St Giles in which he stayed during the Plague still stands and is now a little museum. There is some period furniture, some pictures and early editions.

The National Portrait Gallery, London contains the poet's portrait as a Cambridge student and many other portraits of the great men of his period.

Index

Addison, Joseph 106
Aeneid (Virgil) 38
Anatomy of Melancholy (Burton) 23
Apology for Smectymnuus (Milton) 36, 68
Arcades (Milton) 53
Aeropagitica (Milton) 9, 23, 28–30, 36, 61, 68, 113
astrology 48
As You Like It (Shakespeare) 86
'At a Vacation Exercise' (Milton) 56
Atheist's Tragedy, The (Tourneur) 84
Aubrey, John 2, 3

Bacon, Francis 45
Bartholomew Fair (Jonson) 84
Baxter, Richard 20–1, 22, 23
Bernini, Gianlorenzo 41
Bible, The, Authorized Version 84; influence on Milton 43, 60–4; prophesies 30–3
Bishops' War 24
Blake, William 75, 110–11, 113
blank verse 92–9
Brontë, Charlotte and Emily 109, 113
Bunyan, John 21, 23, 81
Burton, Robert 16–17, 23
Byron, Lord 109, 113

Calvin, John 21
Calvinism 21–3
Catholicism 20, 25
Chain of Being, The 49–50
Charles I 4, 8, 18, 19, 20, 24, 27
Christ's College, Cambridge 5–6
Cipolla, Carlo 17
Civil War 8–10, 24, 28
Commonwealth, Milton's service to 33–5
Comus (Milton) 42, 65, 87–8, 91–2, 99
Cooper, Thomas 111
Copernicus 47
Cowley, Abraham 61
Cowper, William 108, 113
Crashaw, Richard 90, 99
Cromwell, Oliver 9, 10, 34, 35

Dance to the Music of Time, A (Poussin) 39–40
Darbyshire, Helen 101
De Doctrina Christiana 26–7, 35, 36, 62, 68, 83
Defensio Secunda pro Populo Anglicano 4, 23, 35, 36, 57, 68
Defence of Poesy 58
Dekker, Thomas 23
Diodati, Charles 7
Doctrine and Discipline of Divorce, The (Milton) 10
Donne, John 65, 68, 84, 89, 99
Dryden, John 54, 55, 106
Dunciad (Pope) 107, 113
Dyer, Thomas 107, 113

Earle, John 23
Early Lives (Richardson) 10, 52, 55, 93, 99
Eclogues (Virgil) 86
editing, problems of 100–105
education, Milton's definition 56
Eikonoclastes (Milton) 35
elements, the four 51, 53
Ellworthy 65

epic, understanding 82–3
European Culture and Overseas Expansion (Cipolla) 17

Faerie Queen, The (Spenser) 38, 55, 57, 81, 83
Faithorne 1
'Fleece, The' (Dyer) 113
freedom: of the press 28; religious 24–30

Galileo, influence on Milton 42, 43, 45
Gill, Alexander 5
Glimpse of Sion's Glory, A (Knollys) 36
'Good-Morrow, The' (Donne) 99
Graves, Robert 112

Higden, Ranulph 55
Hill, Christopher 15–17, 23
History of Britain, The (Milton) 35
History of the World, The (Raleigh) 84
'Holy Sonnet XIV' (Donne) 99
Homer 43, 60
Hooker, Richard 78, 83
'Hope' (Cowper) 113
'Hymn to God my God in Sicknesse' (Donne) 68
'Hymn of the Nativity' (Crashaw) 99
Hyperion (Keats) 111

'Il Penseroso' (Milton) 53, 55
Instrument of Government (1653) 26, 27, 36
Itinerary (Moryson) 23

James I 18, 20
Jonson, Ben 65, 84, 92

Keats, John 111
Knollys, Hanser 31

'L'Allegro' (Milton) 87, 91, 99
Landscape with a Snake (Poussin) 40, 89
Langland, William 80
Lara (Byron) 113
Laud, Archbishop 20, 24, 25, 26, 31
Language Poets Use, The (Nowottny) 96
London 11–15
Lorrain, Claude 88, 89
'Lycidas' (Milton) 87, 90–1, 99, 103, 104, 105
Lyrical Ballads (Wordsworth) 109

man, origins 50–2
Manso, J. B. 38
Marriage of Heaven and Hell, The (Blake) 111
Marvell, Andrew 10
Mercury and Battus (Lorrain) 88, 89
Micosmographie (Earle) 23
Metaphysical poets 89–91, 111
Millennium, The 30–3
Midsummer Night's Dream, A (Shakespeare) 91
Milton, John: ambitions 7, 57–9; background: cultural 84, economic and social 11–17, family 4, London 11–15, political 18–19, religious 19–23; biographies 1–4; blindness 4, 10, 69, 99, 100; on divorce 9, 28, 33; education 5–6; influences: biblical 43, 60–4; classical 43–4, 59–62, 98, Elizabethan 84–9, Italian 37–42, Metaphysicals 89–91, Shakespearean 91–2; Italian travels 7–8; on liberty 23; marriages 8–10; politics 4, 9–10; portraits 1–3; private studies 7; radicalism 5–6; Reformation papers 8, 31–3; subsequent influence 106–13
Milton (Blake) 113
(Tillyard) 61
Monteverdi 42
Moryson, Fynes 23
music: influence on Milton 42; of the spheres 52–4

Nowottny, Winifred 96

'Ode on the Morning of Christ's Nativity' 3, 90, 99
Of Education (Milton) 68
Of the Laws of Ecclesiastical Politie (Hooker) 83
Of Reformation Touching Church Discipline in England (Milton) 36, 68
'On the Death of a Fair Infant' (Milton) 84–5, 99
On Time (Milton) 99
Ovid 60, 85

Paradise Lost (Milton): allegory, use 80–2, 98; Angels, fall 77–8; beginning and ending 69–70; editing 100–105; Fall, The 65–8; general points 1, 4, 10, 24, 27, 28, 30, 35, 38, 39, 40–2, 44–8, 53, 54, 58, 59, 61–2, 65, 69–83, 88, 91, 92, 106, 107, 109, 110; God, portrayal 76–7; Heaven and Hell 78–9; oratory and invective 93–4; subject choice 65; syntax 94–8; theme 72; tree of knowledge 73–6
Paradise Regained (Milton) 2, 10, 24, 65, 69–72, 99
Passions, The 54–5, 59
pastoral convention 86–9
Petition of Right (1628) 18–19
Phillips, Edward 4, 8–9
Piers Plowman (Langland) 80
Pilgrim's Progress 21–2, 23, 26, 81
Plato 58
Poetical Works of John Milton, The (Darbyshire) 101
poetry: nature of 58–9; religious content 87
Polychronicon (Higden) 55
Pope, Alexander 107
Poussin, Nicholas 39–40, 89
Presbyterianism 24–6
Prometheus Unbound (Shelley) 113
Ptolemaic system 45–7, 78
Puritanism 19–23, 25–7
Pythagoras 53

Raleigh, Sir Walter 84
Raphael 45
Ready and Easy Way to Establish a Free Commonwealth (Milton) 10, 35
Reason 54–5
Reason of Church Government, The (Milton) 36, 59, 68
Reformation to Industrial Revolution (Hill) 23
Religion and the Rise of Capitalism (Tawney) 23
Relinquae Baxterianae 23
Restoration 35–6
Richardson, Jonathan 2, 4, 52
romantic poetry 109–11

Samson Agonistes (Milton) 2, 10, 89, 92, 99
science, influence on Milton 44–8
Seven Deadly Sins of London, The (Dekker) 23
Seventeenth Century Background, The (Willey) 55, 68
Shakespeare, William: general 65, 84, 86, 111; influence on Milton 91–2
Shelley, Mary 109
Shelley, Percy Bysshe 109
Shepheards Calendar (Spenser) 86–7
Sidney, Sir Philip 58
similes, extended 98
'Song for St Cecilia's Day, A' (Dryden) 55
Spectator, The 106
Spenser, Edmund 38, 49, 57, 80, 81, 85, 86–7, 90
spirit 52
State of England, The (Wilson) 23

Tasso, Torquato 38
Tawney, R. H. 22
Tempest, The (Shakespeare) 84
Tenure of Kings and Magistrates (Milton) 9, 34, 36
Third Prolusion (Milton) 6
Tillyard, Dr. E. M. W. 61
Tourneur, Cyril 84
'The Tower' 113

Uniformity, Act of 20

Virgil 38, 43, 60, 86

Willey, Basil 55, 64, 68, 76, 83
Wilson, Thomas 20, 23
Winter's Tale, The (Shakespeare) 84
Wood, Anthony à 3
Wordsworth, William 109
Wuthering Heights (Brontë) 109, 113

Yeats, W. B. 113

S. MARTIN'S COLLEGE OF EDUCATION · LANCASTER ·